In Praise
of the
Inexpressible

In Praise of the Inexpressible

PAUL'S EXPERIENCE OF THE DIVINE MYSTERY

JEAN PAILLARD

translated from the original Swedish by
Richard J. Erickson

HENDRICKSON PUBLISHERS

© 2003 by Jean Paillard

Hendrickson Publishers, Inc.
P. O. Box 3473
Peabody, Massachusetts 01961-3473

ISBN 1-56563-734-8

Original edition published in Swedish under the title: *Till det osägbaras lov* by Bokförlaget Libris, Örebro, Sweden. Copyright © Bokförlaget Libris.

Printed in the United States of America

First Printing — November 2003

Library of Congress Cataloging-in-Publication Data

Paillard, Jean, 1921–
    [Till det osgbaras lov. English]
    In praise of the inexpressible : Paul's experience of the divine mystery / Jean Paillard ; translated from Swedish by Richard J. Erickson.
        p. cm.
    ISBN 1-56563-734-8 (alk. paper)
    1. Bible. N.T. Epistles of Paul—Theology. 2. Paul, the Apostle, Saint. I. Title.
    BS2651.P27213 2003
    227'.06—dc22
                                                2003015559

To everyone of good will.

Table of Contents

Foreword

The Apostle Paul and I are like two old sparring partners. I have fought with him for decades, and I have written about him as I have seen fit. In recent years, though, he has been sending me new signals, signals that at first I found difficult to interpret. Words and images rose urgently to my attention every time I reread his letters, and I had difficulty in identifying a common denominator among them.

Eventually I realized that Paul was weary of being regarded as a sly debater, the indefatigable but occasionally tedious disputant, the obnoxious sort of person who felt compelled to reply to any argument no matter what it might cost him.

I began to search for texts that revealed another side of his personality, and, to my great surprise, I discovered a good deal of them—some meditative, some lyrical. All these texts reflect his spontaneous response to highly personal experiences of the deepest dimension of reality.

Although texts such as these have "been there" all along, we have largely ignored them. But I gradually came to see that they correspond precisely to what I myself have been longing for, a sense of the mystical. So, with pen in hand, I struggled to understand them. My hope now is that this book, which is a result of these struggles, will help other people, believers or not, to rethink their views of Paul and to plunge resolutely with him into the depth and richness of the divine mystery.

Stockholm, Advent 2000
Jean Paillard

Before the divine
the strongman stands broken.

Friedrich Hölderlin

You are as human as anyone else is.

Gunnar Ekelöf

It is important
—not to make any divine idols;
—not to make an idol of who God is, or of what he wants;
—not to make a theology;

. . .

Lars Gyllensten

Part One

A Heightened Sense of Smell,
A Loss of Sight

Chapter 1

A Fragrance of Christ
2 Corinthians 2:14–16

Someone says something indisputably true and well articulated, but no one responds to it. Someone else may say the very same thing, and everyone responds. How is it possible that people can behave so differently in reaction to the very same message? The explanation is perhaps that the first speaker communicates nothing but a doctrine, whereas the second communicates a personal experience. This second speaker conveys something not merely true in its own right, but something true and significant to her, the speaker. And for that reason, the listener can experience it as important to him as well.

This phenomenon, relevant as it is to the relationship between a speaker and a listener, applies equally well to the relationship between a writer and a reader. Consider the fairly well known Paul of Tarsus, who wrote a number of famous letters. Does he communicate in them a doctrine, or an experience, or both? And what is the difference between them?

DOCTRINE AND EXPERIENCE

Any systematically developed way of thinking is conditioned by a particular time and culture. It can be as easily dated as a style of architecture, and it becomes antiquated just as readily. The imagery used for describing an experience is likewise time-bound and culturally conditioned. But the experience itself, if it is sufficiently profound, may prove timeless and universal. In such cases, the person who actually says, "This happened to me," could say just as well, "This happened to us, to all of us." That person stands in as a representative for everyone.

We formulate a doctrine with the help of well-defined concepts. The result is more or less unambiguous, relatively flat and two-dimensional. An experience, by contrast, is many-sided, three-dimensional. It is thus richer than a teaching; in a certain sense it may even be indescribable.

A doctrine is obedient to the one who frames it. He puts it together from the outside, systematically shaping the ideas toward a goal he consciously holds in mind. But an experience obeys no one. It occurs unannounced and afterward is not so easily accounted for. It runs on ahead of us, so to speak, and we try in vain to keep up with it. We fabricate our doctrinal systems, but our experiences shape us and drive us onward where we would not have expected to go.

We can familiarize ourselves with a doctrine. It may engage our interest, though as a rule we try to maintain a certain distance from it. But a life experience engages our entire being, mind and heart alike.

Through assimilating a new doctrine, we merely add to the bulk of our knowledge. An encounter with a personal experience, however, deepens our insight. The essence of a person thus does not consist in the ideas she entertains—these she can manipulate at will. The essence of a person consists in what she has experienced. We need to keep this in mind as we consider the Apostle Paul.

A JOYFUL OUTBURST

We know that in his younger days Paul was a brilliant student of the famous rabbi Gamaliel (Acts 22:3). We often speak of Paul's great learning. We write books about his Christology, his soteriology, and his ecclesiology. We analyze the various concepts he employed: grace, reconciliation, justification, and others. Yet Paul was no desk-bound theologian. He was a frontline missionary. He was a spiritual guide, one who dealt personally with real flesh-and-blood people. He spoke with them openly regarding the foundation of his own life. His expositions are nicely structured, to be sure, but their most important feature, their central nerve, is the vital insight pervading all his writings. These are no mere intellectual discussions. Paul was genuinely inspired as he dictated his letters, and the most valuable thing about them is their spirit. Something in them breathes out confidence, hope, and a feeling of ultimate victory.

We often discuss Paul's "theology" (perhaps too often!), but he himself used a different word for referring to what he wished to communicate. Far more frequently than any other New Testament writer, he speaks of "the gospel," a word originally implying good news, dynamic and loaded with feeling, better than mere information. How can a message of such joy be most effectively expressed? Can a purely objective description do it justice?

Let's go back in time to 56 or 57 C.E. Some time earlier, while in far off Ephesus, Paul receives alarming news from

Corinth concerning the congregation he established there in 51 C.E. This church leaves a lot to be desired in its behavior and teaching. From Ephesus, where he has been residing since 53, Paul writes the Corinthians a preliminary letter, mentioned in 1 Corinthians 5:9 but now lost. Since this letter brings about little change in the conditions in the church, no more than a brief visit would have done (2 Cor 12:14), he then sends Timothy with instructions to clear up the situation (1 Cor 4:17).

Eventually the Corinthians write to Paul with a list of questions. He answers them in a new letter, the one we know as 1 Corinthians, written probably in 55 C.E. Soon afterward, Paul sends Titus to this Greek port city. Titus is a skillful arbitrator, but he can only confirm that the state of affairs is intractable. He reports that neither Paul's two letters nor Timothy's visit has achieved the desired effect.

Paul now sends the Corinthians a third letter, written "in much distress and anguish of heart" (2 Cor 2:3–4; 7:8–9). This letter, like the first one, is also lost. To relieve his distress, he sends out Titus again, with the same mission as before, to restore order. Paul waits impatiently in Ephesus for fresh news of the difficult congregation. Finally, forced by circumstances to leave Ephesus, he travels north to Troas in the hope of meeting Titus there on his way back. But Paul can find no peace of mind in Troas, since Titus does not appear (2 Cor 2:12–13). He therefore moves on to Macedonia, where at last Titus arrives, bringing good news. "He told us of your longing, your mourning, your zeal for me," writes Paul in a new letter, the fourth one, which we now know as 2 Corinthians (2 Cor 7:7).

At last he can sigh with relief. The hour of reconciliation has come. Comfort beyond all expectation brings from him a cry of joy. His words of exaltation apparently no longer stand in their original position in the letter, but they deserve a closer examination nonetheless:

But thanks be to God, who in Christ always leads us in triumphal procession, and through us spreads in every place the fragrance that comes from knowing him. (2 Cor 2:14)

A FRAGRANCE OF CHRIST

Why does Paul speak of a fragrance? On the one hand, any scientific hypothesis can be interesting; it can satisfy our curiosity. But a merely scientific hypothesis lacks "aroma." We can say the same thing about a theological construction. Wisdom, on the other hand, gives off a pleasant scent, which is why Paul does not hesitate to compare that most sublime faculty of human understanding with the sense of smell, the most animal of senses, the one that betrays that we are relatives with the ordinary dog.

Nor is Paul content with saying only that he is spreading a fragrance of knowledge. He actually says that he himself *is* a fragrance. "For we are the aroma *(euōdia)* of Christ to God among those who are being saved and among those who are perishing; to the one a fragrance *(osmē)* from death to death, to the other a fragrance from life to life" (2 Cor 2:15–16). We are all familiar with how Paul debates and polemicizes, how he presses home his arguments in his attempt to convince both Jews and Greeks. Still, in the end, he compares his apostolic calling with the diffusing of a fragrance. A scent is perceptible, whether sweet or foul. When lilacs are in bloom, we do not need to see them. We sense they are there, and all the more so after dark. The darkness itself becomes a perfume, and we experience lilacs as an invisible presence in the night.

A fragrance is also a bare, solitary phenomenon. Flowers grow in a garden or on a meadow, and that is all they have to do. We don't need to read through a set of instructions on their use or consult some learned essay on the laws of smell. All we need to do is to draw in a deep breath full of the life-giving scent. Paul feels justified in using this image, because he has confidence in the ability of the truth, like a flower, to do its work without his help. He refuses to appeal to external support, as he is quick to point out (2 Cor 3:1). Instead, he builds his case on the power of the naked word.

Paul also speaks of a fragrance of Christ "from life to life." The one leads to the other. In one respect, of course, Christianity is a doctrine, something that must be proclaimed, explained, and defended. This is both its strength and its weakness—perhaps in our day, primarily its weakness. We are wearied unto death by a host of opinion mongers who peddle their theories in a noisy strip-mall of ideas. Each of them claims to be worthy of our allegiance and strives to out-shout the competition. Tired of this din, worn out from having to listen to so many arguments and counter-arguments, we gradually long for a more immediate form of communication. We are ready to listen to a soft-spoken preacher, someone just like Paul in his better moments. He compares the effect he makes on people with the effect made by a fragrance. It is invisible, yet fully perceptible; something subtle that insinuates itself who knows how. In short, it is something over which we have no control.

It can hardly be disputed that in the end we make a greater impression through what we are than through what we say. Communication of the faith is an epidemic phenomenon; faith spreads itself like an infection, or better, like a fragrance "from life to life." The truth-seeker follows his nose, so to speak, back to Christ, the source, back to him who is the essence of life itself.

It was precisely to this spiritual sense of smell that Ambrose, the fourth-century bishop of Milan, referred when he explained to newly baptized adults why he touched their nostrils during the baptismal ceremony. The meaning of this ritual gesture, he told them, was that they might always be able to catch the scent of their Savior.

Down through the ages other great writers, and even some not so great, have likewise used the sense of smell to illustrate the intuition for an elusive reality. Writers still do this in our day. A case in point is C. S. Lewis's modern classic, the Chronicles of Narnia (1950–1956), written for children but secretly enjoyed by adults, too. The stories concern a magnificent lion named Aslan, who is quite obviously meant to remind readers of Christ. In the first book of the series, *The Lion, the Witch and the Wardrobe,* Lewis alludes to Aslan's natural powers of attraction. "At the name of Aslan each one of the children felt something jump in his inside. . . . Susan felt as if some delicious smell or some delightful strain of music had just floated by her."

Other writers have occupied themselves with the wordless allure that religious realities can exert over us. In a private letter to a friend in 1956, the young Swedish poet Tomas Tranströmer says of himself that he feels like "a detective at the beginning of an investigation." Further on in the letter he speaks of the Truth as a puzzle to be solved, and toward the end he mentions French mystery writer Georges Simenon's hero, Commissaire Maigret. With good reason, detectives are sometimes called bloodhounds, hunting dogs that track down game with their noses. It is no accident that the word *spår* ("traces") appears some ten years later in the title of Tranströmer's 1966 collection of poetry, *Klanger och spår* ("Sounds and Traces"). The volume includes a poem called "Hommages," or "tributes," in which the authors he celebrates include Simenon himself: "We locked ourselves in with Simenon / and breathed in the smells of human life." Quite logically this section of the poem concludes with the admonition, "Know the smell of the truth!" This exhortation is echoed in a later poem: "Go like a bloodhound where the truth has gone."

Novelist Irmelin Sandman-Lilius uses the same approach in her story *Främlingsstjärnan* (1980). At a certain point in the narrative a poet, Rudolf Aronius, is conversing with his friend Ellen. She says, "I can't say what it is I believe; I can only say what I don't believe." To this Aronius replies, "Mystery! Mystery! . . . We understand nothing. That's clear enough. . . . We can only try to sniff our way along with our spiritual noses." The Apostle Paul is thus not the only one who includes the sense of smell among our powers of religious perception. In a day of shallow rationalism, it is well worth rehabilitating this intuitive notion of understanding.

A CELEBRATED VICTOR

When Paul speaks of a fragrance of Christ, we gather that he experienced Christ with the same pleasure he found in smelling something lovely. In other words, he must have found Christ attractive in some way. But in what way? And what led Paul the Jew to use this particular image in describing his attraction?

In the ancient Middle East, costly perfumes and sweet-smelling spices played a big role in both profane and religious life. The Old Testament is rich in texts that connect them with various festivities. In well-to-do homes it was customary to sprinkle beds and clothing with myrrh, aloe, and cassia (Ps 45:8; Prov 7:17). Exquisite scents were believed to express and increase the joy of living: "Perfume and incense make the heart glad" (Prov 27:9). Before a banquet, a man would apply the finest ointment to his body (Amos 6:6), and a host would anoint his guest's head with balsam (Ps 23:5; cf. Luke 7:36, 46).

Fragrance is also sometimes associated with the respect and good reputation a person enjoys. This can be true either of an individual or of a group, collectively personified, such as when the Lord says of his people, "I will be like the dew to Israel; he shall blossom like the lily . . . his beauty shall be like the olive tree, and his fragrance like that of Lebanon" (Hos 14:5–6).

At other times, fragrance is linked with a prepossessing appearance. The lovers in Song of Solomon never tire of comparing each other's charms with pleasant smells. From the very outset, the young woman exclaims, "Your anointing oils are fragrant, your name is perfume poured out; therefore the maidens love you" (Song 1:3). Her beloved employs the same symbols to sing the praises of her physical attractions: "Your lips distill nectar, my bride; honey and milk are under your tongue; the scent of your garments is like the scent of Lebanon. . . . Your channel is an orchard of pomegranates with all choicest fruits, henna with nard, nard and saffron, calamus and cinnamon, with all trees of frankincense, myrrh and aloes, with all chief spices" (Song 14:11–14).

The ancient Jews did not readily admit the Song of Solomon into the canon of their scriptures. Its open sensuality shocked them. Eventually, however, they justified the recognition of this love song by interpreting it allegorically. The highly praised young man is God and the lovely object of his affection is his people Israel, or perhaps the individual believer. The decision to canonize the Song of Solomon, delayed as it was, reflected a remarkable insight. The guardians of Jewish scripture realized that no human relationship is rich enough for symbolizing the intimate relationship between God and humanity, and that eager curiosity, wonder, fascination, even lust, have their place in the life of faith.

Particularly relevant for this subject of the fragrance of knowledge is what the Old Testament has to say about divine wisdom, often symbolized by a woman, Lady Sophia. The author of the Wisdom of Sirach presents her as praising herself in the following words:

> Like cassia and camel's thorn I gave forth perfume,
> and like choice myrrh I spread my fragrance,
> like galbanum, onycha, and stacte,
> and like the odor of incense in the tent. (Sir 24:15)

In this way she alludes to the secret signals she sends to those who seek the truth, in the hope that they will succumb to her subtle allure. Further on, she turns to her listeners with a summons:

> Listen to me, my faithful children, and blossom
> like a rose growing by a stream of water.
> Send out fragrance like incense,
> and put forth blossoms like a lily.
> Scatter the fragrance, and sing a hymn of praise;
> bless the Lord for all his works. (Sir 39:14–15)

"Scatter the fragrance!" urges Lady Sophia. This is exactly what that son of wisdom, Paul, claims to be doing when he spreads a fragrance of knowledge (2 Cor 2:14)—but knowledge about what precisely? A parallel, complementary image in the same verse can put us on the trail to the answer. The apostle states that God is leading him, through Christ, in his triumphal procession. The technical term he uses here—*thriambeuonti*—originally had to do with the victory march of a conquering general on his return to the imperial capital. Slaves or soldiers would burn sweet-smelling herbs in advance of his approach. The Christ who, through his apostle, spreads a sweet fragrance is thus the conquering Christ. But in what sense is he a conqueror?

GOD'S ABIDING SPLENDOR

In spite of the good news Titus has brought him, Paul still feels the need to defend himself one more time. It is unlikely that all his opponents have suddenly dropped their weapons. He points out therefore that he serves God's purposes "in Christ" (2 Cor 2:17). In an almost conversational tone, he insists that he has no need to legitimate himself in the usual way:

> Are we beginning to commend ourselves again? Surely we do not need, as some do, letters of recommendation to you or from you, do we? You yourselves are our letter, written on our hearts, to be known and read by all; and you show that you are a letter of Christ, prepared by us, written not with ink but with the Spirit of the living God, not on tablets of stone but on tablets of human hearts. (2 Cor 3:1–3)

The point of this is that the very existence of the congregation at Corinth, founded by Paul himself, is all the proof of apostolic legitimacy he needs.

The contrast between, on the one hand, a dead text written on papyrus or inscribed on stone, and, on the other hand, a living reality inscribed on a human heart, leads Paul to draw yet another comparison. God, he says, "has made us competent to be ministers of a new covenant, not of letter but of spirit; for the letter kills, but the Spirit gives life" (2 Cor 3:6). In order to emphasize the special nature of this new covenant and its superiority, he compares it with the old covenant in several different ways. But the essential distinction between the two covenants is "glory," a key word occurring fifteen times in this context (3:7–8; 4:1–6, 17). Paul writes:

> Now if the ministry of death, chiseled in letters on stone tablets [the tablets of the law], came in glory so that the people of Israel could not gaze at Moses' face because of the glory of his face, a glory now set aside, how much more will the ministry

> of the Spirit come in glory? For if there was glory in the min-
> istry of condemnation, much more does the ministry of justifi-
> cation abound in glory! Indeed, what once had glory has lost
> its glory because of the greater glory; for if what was set aside
> came through glory, much more has the permanent come in
> glory! (2 Cor 3:7–11)

Paul follows a method of reasoning common in his culture, ar-
guing from a lesser point to a greater. He starts from the account of Moses' most significant experience, described in the
Book of Exodus:

> Moses came down from Mount Sinai. As he came down from
> the mountain with the two tablets of the covenant in his hand,
> Moses did not know that the skin of his face shone because he
> had been talking with God. When Aaron and all the Israelites
> saw Moses, the skin of his face was shining, and they were
> afraid to come near him. But Moses called to them; and Aaron
> and all the leaders of the congregation returned to him, and
> Moses spoke with them. . . . When Moses had finished speak-
> ing with them, he put a veil on his face. (Exod 34:29–33)

This text relates the story of Moses' great privilege, which is the
greatest privilege anyone could possibly imagine. Yet it is as if
the patriarch of the old covenant had not been glorified at all in
comparison with the overwhelming glory of the new covenant
(2 Cor 3:10). For the radiance of his face gradually disap-
peared, while the glory of the new covenant endures (vv. 7, 11).
It is worth noticing that the comparison is incomplete. Once
Paul mentions Moses, we expect that he will immediately ad-
duce a second historical figure to represent the new covenant
and to reflect the greater the glory of Yahweh. But, for now at
least, he does not do so.

To this point Paul has built his argument on the story in
Exodus, where Moses, out of consideration for the Israelites'
terror, put a mask or a veil over his face (2 Cor 3:7–11). In the
following verses (vv. 12–18), he appeals to a later rabbinic tradition that explains the veil differently. According to this explanation, the veil's purpose is not to conceal the intolerable
intensity of the radiance—its strength, therefore—but to conceal its transitory character—its weakness:

> Since, then, we have such a hope [in an abiding glory], we act
> with great boldness, not like Moses, who put a veil over his face
> to keep the people of Israel from gazing at the end of the glory
> that was being set aside. But their minds were hardened. In-
> deed, to this very day, when they hear the reading of the old
> covenant, that same veil is still there, since only in Christ is it
> set aside. Indeed, to this very day whenever Moses is read, a
> veil lies over their minds; but when one turns to the Lord, the
> veil is removed. (2 Cor 3:12–16)

At this point the text becomes difficult to interpret. Based
on a thorough study of the material, A. Feuillet proposes the
following translation:

> And all of us, who without veils over our faces behold in a mir-
> ror [i.e., in Christ] the Lord's [God's] glory, are being trans-
> formed to his image, and thus we are led from glory unto glory
> through the Lord who is the Spirit. (2 Cor 3:18)

According to the rabbinic tradition Paul appeals to here, Moses
hid his face with a cloth "so that the Israelites would not see
how what was passing away actually vanished." According to
the apostle's own interpretation, a veil remains over their descendants, his own contemporaries, when the old covenant's
scriptures are read in the synagogue on the Sabbath. Indeed, he
writes, "to this very day . . . a veil lies over their minds." The
reason for this is that the veil lying over their hearts is removed

only through Christ (vv. 14b–16). And so here, for the first
time, he names the figure who stands in contrast to Moses.

But to judge from what he now writes, hardness of heart
affects not only the Jews of his day, but all nonbelievers as well.
"And even if our gospel is veiled, it is veiled to those who are
perishing. In their case the god of this world [the devil] has
blinded the minds of the unbelievers [without exception], to
keep them from seeing the light of the gospel of the glory of
Christ, who is the image of God" (4:3–4). Their fate is truly
tragic: "they are perishing." If this sounds familiar, it is because
Paul has already mentioned, in connection with his words
about fragrance, that there are "those who are perishing"
(2:15). In the same way, prisoners of war faced execution at the
end of the victorious general's triumphal march. For such as
these, Christianity is "a fragrance [or perhaps better a fume, or
a foul odor] of death to death" (2:16).

For those who put their trust in Christ, however, the veil is
lifted when they turn to him (2 Cor 3:16). From henceforth, they
are led "from one degree of glory to another." At first sight, these
words may sound naively optimistic, as if a believer experiences
nothing but one brilliant success after another. What is intended, in fact, is something quite different: a progressive transformation. It is almost what Paul earlier spoke of as "a fragrance
from life to life" (2:16), or what he will later refer to, in his letter
to the Romans, as going "from faith to faith" (Rom 1:17). The
thought is this: the more we behold God's glory, the more we are
shaped by it. The believer who gazes at this glory is soon transformed through this very act of gazing. One can scarcely place a
higher value on religious contemplation than this.

For those who believe, from whose faces the veil has been
lifted, the fragrance of Christ is thus "fragrance from life to

life," leading them to salvation (2 Cor 2:16). Recognizing and learning to appreciate the fragrance of Christ is consequently synonymous with "seeing the light of the gospel of the glory of Christ, who is the image of God" (4:4). They belong together. And it is precisely by contemplating God's glory, as reflected in Christ, that believers are transformed gradually into his likeness.

THE GLORY OF THE RISEN ONE

We are approaching the end of Paul's long argument, the culmination of his progressively intensified rationale. We have seen God's glory reflected in Moses (2 Cor 3:7), then in the Christians (3:18), and finally in Christ, who is actually the immediate source of the others' glory (4:4). Here we must raise one last question: What exactly does the phrase "glory of Christ" mean in the last cited verse? The answer appears in the final section of Paul's exposition:

> For we do not proclaim ourselves; we proclaim Jesus Christ as Lord and ourselves as your slaves for Jesus' sake. For it is the God who said, "Let light shine out of darkness," who has shone in our hearts to give the light of the knowledge of the glory of God in the face of Jesus Christ. (2 Cor 4:5–6)

When and how does God's glory shine forth from the face of Christ? Paul presents the gospel here in categories of light. But why does he do so? The Jews readily dealt in just such categories in order to describe the brilliance of God's loftiness. Yet Paul the rabbi is not simply dependent on his forefathers' tradition when he portrays his calling as he does. He is also reacting spontaneously, out of the experience of his own life.

On the threshold of the new creation, which he will soon mention (2 Cor 5:17), Paul describes his spiritual rebirth with the help of the narrative of the first creation, or more precisely the creation of light. When did God enlighten his heart? It was when he was on the road to Damascus. Suddenly he found himself surrounded by a blinding light from heaven (Acts 9:3; 22:6). There the glory of God shone upon him, radiating from the face of the Risen Christ. The reality of this experience brought it about that the persecutor of the church changed sides.

From this day forth, Paul is fascinated, nearly besotted, with the radiance of the Risen One, whom he experiences as triumphant. He is virtually beside himself with joy whenever he learns that his preaching of Christ's glory or his spreading of Christ's fragrance (they are one and the same) is going forward successfully. "But thanks be to God, who in Christ always leads us in triumphal procession, and through us spreads in every place the fragrance that comes from knowing him" (2 Cor 2:14). In this he seems to be alluding to a detail of the Roman practice of victory celebration. If the conquering general had sons, it was customary for him to let them accompany him in his chariot or to let them ride on the horses that drew it. A general bringing his sons along in a triumphal procession was thus a fitting image for what God does with his apostle when the apostle is successful in his mission.

Chapter 2

Three Days without Sight

Acts 9:1–9; 22:6–11; 26:9–18; Galatians 1:12–17

A Jesus Christ who is certain of victory, a risen and glorified Christ whose face reflects the glory of God and who therefore becomes a visual feast for his apostle and all his adherents—it sounds utterly beautiful, even sublime. But is it true? It is characteristic of Christianity that as a religion it is anchored in history, in the concrete and the everyday. In fact, a large portion of the New Testament consists of narratives. The authors claim to report actual events, not least the resurrection of Christ, on which Christianity stands or falls. "If Christ has not been raised, then our proclamation has been in vain and your faith has been in vain," writes Paul to the Corinthian church (1 Cor 15:14). Indeed, he is personally convinced that the resurrected Christ revealed himself to him not far from the city of Damascus.

How valid is this conviction? What actually did happen to Paul outside the gates of the Syrian city? Luke considered the event important enough to report it no fewer than three times in the Acts of the Apostles. These three texts deserve a close examination, and although it may be a bit tedious, it is necessary to do this if we wish to avoid depending on mere pious notions.

This should be a critical investigation as well, since there are certain disturbing features in Luke's account. It teems with supernatural phenomena, including three visions in just two days, occurring in and around Damascus. That is no small number! Are we to believe that Paul and his circle of acquaintances occupied a kind of fairy wonderland? Even if we do not a priori reject supernatural events as such, we have every reason to be surprised at their frequency here and to test their historical veracity through careful reflection.

This critical reflection is all the more justified because of a number of irregularities in Luke's work. Jacques Dupont, Gerhard Lohfink, and other researchers have demonstrated, namely, that Luke's three successive narratives of the Damascus event do not entirely agree with one another. We are warranted, then, in playing detective or trial judge, and in cross-examining the witnesses. Doubt is a prerequisite of faith.

THREE INCONSISTENT ACCOUNTS

According to the first version of the story, Paul's traveling companions hear a voice but do not see the speaker (Acts 9:7); according to the second version, they see a light, but do not hear the voice (22:9). In the first account, they remain standing, dumbstruck, while Paul alone falls to the ground (9:7); in the third account, everyone falls down (26:14). In the first two tellings, the only instruction Paul receives is to enter Damascus. Once there, he will be told what he must do. And sure enough, in the continuation of the story (9:10–19a; 22:12–16), we hear that he is taken in hand by a certain Ananias, who informs him of his coming mission among the gentiles. But according to the third version of the story, it is Christ himself who sends Paul out to the pagan world (26:16–18). In at least three places, then, these accounts of the story diverge from one another, which, in terms of historical authenticity, does not bode well. Is it not possible that Luke, who was not actually there himself, simply invented these accounts?

It is awkward enough that the Book of Acts exhibits its own internal contradictions. Yet certain particulars deposited there also do not agree with details we have in Paul's letters, which, we might add, predate Luke's work. In his epistle to the Galatians, Paul energetically vindicates his calling, insisting that he received it directly from God (Gal 1:1, 12). He means, of course, that there was no human intermediary involved. But to hear Luke tell the story, in the first two versions at least, Paul remained ignorant of God's plan until Ananias informed him of it. Paul himself, we may suppose, ought to know which it was! Does this then mean that Luke is wrong?

And there is another thing. In Acts 9 Luke the narrator tells the story from the outside, so to speak, in the third person ("Now as he was going along and approaching Damascus . . ."). In the following two versions, however, Luke has Paul speaking in his own defense, first before the agitated crowd at the Jerusalem temple (ch. 22), and later before King Agrippa, in the fortress at Caesarea (ch. 26). But in his own letters, Paul does not treat the subject in the same detailed way as Luke portrays him doing in these two texts. Paul surely had a very good reason to render a fully orbed account of this decisive event; namely, he was defending his apostolic mission (e.g., Gal 1:15). Even so, he mentions it only in the briefest way, almost in passing. As a rule he does not like to talk about the visions and revelations he has experienced (e.g., 2 Cor 12:1–4). It is therefore hardly credible that, in speaking publicly at Jerusalem and Caesarea, he would have expressed himself differently from the way he does in the letters he wrote in Ephesus, or anywhere else. This gives us yet another reason to ask probing questions about Luke's versions of the story.

In accordance with the literary conventions current in our culture, we take it for granted that Luke ought to have written just as we ourselves would do. That is, we presume that Luke would have strictly respected the actual sequence of events, almost as if he were compiling a police report. We expect that he would have faithfully reproduced, word for word, the actual speeches he reports. But this he most certainly does not do. As a matter of fact, he allows himself a level of freedom we find shocking. How can he do so? Nowhere does he programmatically describe or justify his procedural methods, but we can deduce what they were by analyzing the literary form and structure of his texts. In other words, we can study the way he writes.

LUKE'S NARRATIVE STRATEGY

As we have seen, two of the Damascus stories are put into Paul's mouth. As it happens, similar speeches (twenty-two in all) make up a full third of the Book of Acts, even though Luke himself could not have heard a single one of them. But all twenty-two are of a particular character. Several peculiarities lead us to regard them at least as the results of heavy editing, if not as literary fictions. As speeches all of them are too short; not one would have lasted more than two or three minutes. Additionally, some would have been virtually incomprehensible to the listeners, who would have been unacquainted with the circumstances Luke describes in the surrounding texts. Yet in other instances, the speaker is portrayed as informing his listeners of something they have already known for some time. Thus these speeches are addressed more to Luke's intended readers than to Paul's actual audiences.

There is more. Most of these speeches are formed on one and the same model. Consider as a first example of this the fact that several times listeners interrupt a speech just as the speaker is about to make the decisive point (e.g., Acts 22:22; 26:24, 28). Here we have a stylistic technique common in the profane literature of the period. As a second example, Luke's speakers—Paul, Peter, or James—often cite the Old Testament, but they do so from the Greek translation, the Septuagint, in spite of the fact that these people actually spoke Aramaic. Here once again, we are dealing with a kind of artificial trick of the trade.

Still another feature worth noticing is a conversational exchange occurring in the reports of the Damascus revelation. In the heart of all three versions of Luke's story, a short dialog between Christ and Paul appears, and always in the same form. First there is a double address and a question: "Saul, Saul! Why are you persecuting me?" (Acts 9:4; 22:7; 26:14). This elicits a counter-question: "Who are you, Lord?" (9:5a; 22:8; 26:15a). Finally comes the answer: "I am Jesus, whom you are persecuting" (9:5b, 22:8, 26:15b). What is remarkable about this exchange is that it has an exact counterpart in several Old Testament texts, and Luke follows the model step by step. He has obviously poured his text into preexistent forms. We did not need even this much to make us suspicious regarding the historical authenticity of the words Luke puts into the mouths of his characters.

Specialists who work with the structural analysis of biblical texts have observed a further perplexing phenomenon. Luke reports two episodes in especially emphatic fashion: Paul's call gets three tellings (as we have seen), and the conversion of the Roman centurion Cornelius gets two (Acts 10:1–11:18). The fact that he reports them more than once indicates the weight he attaches to them. It makes us want to know more about how he pursues his craft.

We read in the first account as follows: "Now there was a
disciple in Damascus named Ananias. The Lord said to him in
a vision, 'Ananias.' He answered, 'Here I am, Lord.' The Lord
said to him, 'Get up and go to the street called Straight, and at
the house of Judas look for a man of Tarsus named Saul. At this
moment he is praying, and he has seen in a vision a man
named Ananias come in and lay his hands on him so that he
might regain his sight'" (Acts 9:10–12). There are two visions
here. The remarkable thing about them is that they are not reported successively, one after the other, but simultaneously, the
one enfolded within the other, like Russian dolls. And they
both have the very same content.

Indeed, the symmetry is truly perfect: Ananias in his
house sees Saul in Judas' house; Saul in Judas' house sees
Ananias in his own house. By itself, this symmetry would not
be sufficient for us to suspect an artificial narrative strategy, had
not Luke in the next chapter made use of the very same model
in his account of Cornelius' conversion. The Roman officer
and Peter, each in his own vision, receive instructions exactly
reflecting the other's (Acts 10:1–23).

The parallelism between the two stories is striking. Does
such perfect symmetry really correspond to the unpredictable
disorder of everyday life? What has happened here is that
Luke, a native Greek author, has borrowed a literary model
that occasionally shows up in his own Hellenistic culture.

This man is a splendid stylist. No one denies it. He truly
has the skill to design a book. With the regularity of clock-
work he alternates shorter and longer speeches with narrative
material. His book's carefully planned construction proceeds,
moreover, with a number of parallelisms and levels of in-

tensification, not least in the Damascus story. Two examples will suffice. The first has to do with Paul's Jewish period. Three times Luke says of him that he opposed the young church. But how does Luke put it? In Acts 9, it is mentioned in an ordinary and summary way, in a subordinate clause: "Saul, still breathing threats and murder against the disciples of the Lord . . ." (9:1). In chapter 22, the observation is made in a somewhat more detailed and concrete way: "I persecuted this Way up to the point of death by binding both men and women and putting them in prison" (22:4).

The third telling is the most detailed of all: "Indeed, I myself was convinced that I ought to do many things against the name of Jesus of Nazareth. And that is what I did in Jerusalem; with authority received from the chief priests, I not only locked up many of the saints in prison, but I also cast my vote against them when they were being condemned to death. By punishing them often in all the synagogues I tried to force them to blaspheme; and since I was so furiously enraged at them, I pursued them even to foreign cities" (Acts 26:9–11). The texts thus get progressively longer, and the level of intensity obviously increases from one to the next.

Another intensification figures just as obviously in the story of Paul's commission to go the gentiles. The universal character of this calling is made increasingly precise with each telling of the tale (from 9:6 to 22:15 to 26:16–18). Once more we have evidence of deft narrative skill. This intensification witnesses to Luke's considerable artistic ability. But this literary beauty also works against him. It can awaken suspicion, almost like make-up applied too carefully. Yet Luke clearly feels right about reediting the documents that have come into his hands, or the traditions he has heard.

With regard to speeches, Luke is not alone in reproducing them freely. A number of historians of that day did the same thing. Even when they had access to the text of the speech their hero actually made, they would quite simply have him make a different speech, one that enabled them to render more effectively the inward sense of what the hero did in fact say. Luke makes their practice a pattern for his own, as we might expect. Still, it makes us a little uncomfortable, and we wonder what confidence we can place in someone who reports events so freely. We cannot answer this question without first posing an - other one: What was Luke's purpose in this? What was he after? Put another way, what literary genre does the Book of Acts belong to? It is important in answering these questions to read Luke in accordance with his own intentions.

LUKE'S PURPOSE

In the preamble to his first volume, the Third Gospel, Luke openly declares his purpose (Luke 1:1–4). But in the preamble to the second volume, he leaves us no clear statement about it. He contents himself by saying simply, "In the first book, Theophilus, I wrote about all that Jesus did and taught from the beginning until the day when he was taken up to heaven, after giving instructions through the Holy Spirit to the apostles whom he had chosen" (Acts 1:1–2). As the Book of Acts unfolds, however, Luke describes how the apostles carry out their master's command and thereby gradually lay the foundations of the church. The book can thus be regarded as the beginning of church history. But what sort of church history is it?

It is clear enough that Luke claims to be reporting facts. What sort of facts, however, is what we wish to determine. In the case of Paul's call, Luke builds upon a firm tradition commonly accepted in the early church. Behind his text, in fact, we catch glimpses of older sources that can be partially reconstructed. He appears moreover to have been informed by the Christians in Judea or in Syria. He is dealing therefore with well-documented data. But he interprets these data. He treats them primarily as a theologian would, highlighting what in his eyes represents their deeper significance. And what primarily interests him is how the young church, step by step, and with considerable difficulty, opened itself to the pagan world. It is no accident that the two episodes to which Luke devotes the greatest space in the book, the conversion of Cornelius and the calling of Paul, both have to do with openness toward the gentiles.

This openness was not automatically assumed, as the early church's long-standing hesitation on the issue bears witness. Luke thus sets out to demonstrate that the openness of the gospel to the gentile world actually represented the will of God. In order to emphasize the divine initiative in this he freely multiplies manifestations and visions. Nor is that all. By stressing Paul's Jewish orthodoxy (Acts 22:3; 26:4f) and by stressing his zealous persecution of the Christians (9:1–2, 13–14, 21; 22:4–5, 19–20; 26:9–11), Luke demonstrates that his hero would never have become a missionary among the gentiles had he been left to do so on his own initiative. To explain such a sudden, unpredictable, and radical conversion, nothing less is needed than an irresistible intervention by God, beginning with the revelation of Christ at Damascus.

Another element pointing to God's initiative in Paul's mission to the gentiles is the use of citations from or allusions to the Old Testament, not least the words Luke places in the mouth of Christ in the third account of Paul's commission (26:15–18). The text is short, four verses only, yet it cites no fewer than three passages in which Ezekiel and Jeremiah describe their own callings, and where Isaiah recounts the calling of the Lord's Servant. In these texts Luke alludes only to the small features that mention sending someone to the gentiles, but this fact itself discloses his intention. By means of these literary structures he wishes to assert the continuity in God's plan of salvation throughout time, a plan that now more than ever concerns the gentiles.

It is time now to separate the wheat from the chaff. What in Luke's text is historically reliable, and what is merely a free literary way of presenting a religious reality?

We can with good reason place a question mark against any number of things. For instance, we can raise questions about the mutually contradictory descriptions of the reactions from Paul's traveling companions, or about Paul's and Ananias's visions of each other. These kinds of phenomena can often be found in ancient literature, and Luke has used them to indicate God's initiative in the persecutor's conversion. Similar skepticism is justified with regard to the literalness of the exchange between Jesus and Paul. Luke himself is responsible for its redaction, this time with the help of Old Testament models. Still another problematic feature is the mission speech attributed to Christ in the third account (Acts 26). There is much to suggest that Paul only later gained clarity regarding his commission to take the gospel beyond the boundaries of Judaism. This speech, then, should be read as Luke's own theological commentary on Paul's being sent out to non-Jews.

All these imaginative reports constitute the literary packaging of a religious message. When we have weeded them out, what remains that can be regarded as strictly historical? In other words, what truly happened to Paul?

WHAT DID PAUL ACTUALLY EXPERIENCE?

One way to get at this is to discern what is common among all three of Luke's accounts and to determine what of that common fund also agrees with the apostle's own testimony in his letters. The first thing we can say with confidence is that the young Saul persecuted the church. Writing later to the Corinthians, Galatians, and Philippians (1 Cor 15:9; Gal 1:13, 23; Phil 3:6), he corroborates what Luke says about his attempt to smother Christianity in its cradle (Acts 9:4–5; 22:7–8; 26:14). In agreement with Luke, he insists that he did so "violently" (Gal 1:13).

A second certainty is that he experienced something that suddenly and radically compelled him to change sides (Acts 9:3, 8, 10; 22:6, 11; 26:19–23). The phenomenal young opponent was transformed 180 degrees into a zealous champion (Gal 1:15–16; 1 Cor 15:8–10). On this point as well, the two men are in agreement.

We come now to the core of the texts, namely that sometime in the mid-30s, Christ revealed himself to the one who would become the Apostle to the Gentiles. For Luke it is clear that Paul has seen the Lord. In the first account of Paul's conversion, he has Ananias say, "Brother Saul, the Lord Jesus, who appeared to you on your way here . . ." (Acts 9:17). Just a bit further on, he has Barnabas describe before the apostles in Jerusalem, "how on the road [Paul] had seen the Lord, who had spoken to him" (Acts 9:27). In the second version, he again has Ananias speaking: "The God of our ancestors has chosen you to know his will, to see the Righteous One and to hear his own voice; for you will be his witness to all the world of what you have seen and heard" (22:14–15). And in the third telling, Jesus himself is made to say, "But get up and stand on your feet; for I have appeared to you for this purpose, to appoint you to serve and testify to the things in which you have seen me and to those in which I will appear to you" (26:16).

All this corroborates what Paul himself writes. In a polemical text from 1 Corinthians, for example, he says, "Have I not seen Jesus our Lord?" (1 Cor 9:1), and then, concluding a list of the appearances of the Risen One, "Last of all, as to one untimely born, he appeared also to me" (15:8). On this fundamental point, Paul thus confirms the tradition reported by Luke. The congruence is all the more remarkable since it appears that Luke had no access to Paul's letters.

A DAZZLING LIGHT

So then, if Christ revealed himself to Paul, the question now becomes how he did it. Hopelessly curious as we are about such details, and giving no thought to how relatively inconsequential they are, we wonder nonetheless how exactly Christ manifested himself. Did he do so by means of an outward, physical phenomenon, one an optician could have measured—at so many vibrations per second? Or did it come as an inward vision? And how did Christ speak, and with what sort of voice, and at how many decibels? A little like nosy children, we want to know these things.

Paul, for his part, is unconcerned with them. Instead he goes right to the heart of the matter. The most urgent thing for him is his radical inner transformation. When we listen to his own words about it, preserved in his letters, and without interference from Luke, we hear him paying special attention to what happened within him, internally. "Christ Jesus has made me his own," he writes to the Philippians (Phil 3:12). He was brutally knocked to the ground, with no possibility of resistance. God determined to "reveal his Son to me," he informs the Galatians (Gal 1:16). God has "shone in [my heart]," he assures the Corinthians (2 Cor 4:6). Everything else is of less significance for him.

Given these circumstances, we can see why Paul never bothers to describe the Risen One. But what does he do instead? According to Luke, he speaks about light, a theme Luke develops more and more sharply and with characteristic skill.

In the first passage he mentions only "a light [*phōs*] from heaven" (9:3). In the second passage he speaks of "a great light" (*phōs hikanon;* 22:6). And in the third version of the story, he sees "a light from heaven, brighter than the sun" (26:13). The progressive intensification is striking. But there is more. In the second and third passages he specifies that the revelation occurred "at midday" (22:6; 26:13), when shadows are at their shortest and the sun's light is at its brightest. In this way, Luke stresses all the more emphatically the brilliance of the heavenly light. The radiance of the vision is so intense that the noonday sun pales by comparison.

More like the sun than the sun itself, it seems. But so much is too much! For the divine light can be dangerous, even fatal. Several Old Testament figures were well aware of this. Moses, for example, begged to see the Lord's glory, but instead got only this in reply: ". . . no one shall see me and live" (Exod 33:20).

According to the tradition Luke used, which (as a tradition) derives chronologically from nearer the actual event, Paul did not die after receiving an overdose of heavenly light, but he did lose his sight for a time. The man who was called to be "a light for the Gentiles" (Acts 13:47), and to "to open their eyes so that they may turn from darkness to light and from the power of Satan to God" (26:18), was himself blinded for the space of three days. "Saul got up from the ground, and though his eyes were open, he could see nothing; so they led him by the hand and brought him into Damascus. For three days he was without sight" (9:8–9). And then, "Since I could not see because of the brightness of that light, those who were with me took my hand and led me to Damascus" (22:11).

Paul's Christian life, therefore, did not begin with a battle of words or a theological debate. It began rather with a devastating event, one that resulted for him in a serious visual impairment. He was rendered completely defenseless against the light emanating from the Risen Christ. This makes good sense, of course. When a gleaming whiteness becomes even whiter, when it becomes as white as it possibly can, everything changes to black. Anyone affected by it can no longer see. The sun is eclipsed itself.

Can we allow ourselves to make such a bold statement? Let us take a quick look at the example of belles-lettres. Poets like to bring extremes into collision with each other, willfully linking together seemingly incompatible, even radically contrasting, elements. They love paradoxes and speak for instance of "frozen fire," or of "a dance without movement," or of "black milk." A paradox is an apparent absurdity. It is a form of play.

Even the church fathers and mystics were poets in their day. They delighted in turns of phrase that perplexed and provoked. They could, for example, speak of a "sober intoxication," in order to characterize the state of a believer who may be spiritually carried away but who simultaneously remains self-controlled. These serious-minded writers did not hesitate to play, least of all when confronted with divine mysteries. They could do so with a perfectly good conscience, since, clearly, playing is a way of refusing to take oneself too seriously, in order thereby to take reality all the more seriously. Play, or paradox, is likewise a way to respect the indescribable. It helps the reader to see that our ordinary rules of language are rendered useless as soon as we find ourselves in the presence of something surpassing all understanding.

Biblical texts sometimes speak of God as making his dwelling in the mists and clouds (e.g., Ps 18:12, repeated in 2 Sam 22:11–12); they portray him as saying to Moses, "I am going to come to you in a dense cloud" (Exod 19:9). Probably influenced by this, some of our spiritual forefathers talk about a "cloud of unknowing." Nicholas of Cusa, who occasionally referred to a "union of opposites," also frequently made use of the expression *docta ignorantia,* that is, a learned nonknowing, or an informed ignorance. With Nicholas, the wise know how not to know. The further they penetrate God's being, the more they discover how deep and fathomless he is, how far beyond all our powers of imagination.

As John of the Cross, for his part, observes in his *Dark Night of the Soul,* "The more the light shines, the more it blinds and darkens the owl's pupil." It is exactly so. An excess of light becomes its own opposite. Everything changes key. Day turns to night. It is what other mystics mean by a "dazzling darkness."

The fact that the divine light is so bright that it paradoxically undoes itself is concretely illustrated in certain old icons. They show the light streaming from God as *black.* Beams of black emanating from the source of light—it sounds preposterous! But it is "truth" just the same. All theology that is not playful and paradoxical is simply bad theology.

Part Two

At the Edge of the Silence

Chapter 3

Fourteen Years in Silence

2 Corinthians 12:1–5

We often judge Paul harshly. We see him as peevish, quarrelsome, and intolerant. Such a verdict is unjust, and for a simple reason. The only thing that has survived from him is a collection of a few letters, written to address a few particular situations. And all of them are of a special character. He sent them whenever he felt compelled to intervene in a congregation going through a crisis or when he felt obliged to correct some misbehavior in which it had indulged. These were necessary, if thankless, duties.

Of all the churches under his jurisdiction, the Corinthian assembly was the most troublesome. We have already noted that the difficulty between Paul and this group lasted for several years, though we have not yet touched on the cause, or causes, of the conflict. It is now time to consider what it was that called forth his reproaches.

A FIRST APOLOGY
2 CORINTHIANS 2:14–7:4

Already in the first letter to Corinth, Paul provides a rather unflattering picture of his problem children. These new, culturally homogeneous Christians really were intolerable. They quarreled constantly, dividing themselves into various cliques and indulging in absurd intellectual posturing, all in order to avoid dealing with more serious scandals. Even so, the tone of the letter is relatively controlled and tranquil.

Much more dramatic is the Second Letter to the Corinthians, and understandably so. Some members of the congregation are slandering Paul in his absence. They accuse Paul of double-crossing them. They upbraid him for his premeditated capriciousness and accuse him of breaking his word. (He had promised to return to them, but had been obliged to change his travel plans and to postpone an upcoming visit.)

Under circumstances like these, he feels constrained to defend himself, and he does so at length in a text that occupies some four chapters in our versions of the Bible (2 Cor 2:14–7:4). There he affirms that he uses no trickery and that he does not falsify the word of God (4:2). He protests that he does not proclaim himself but Jesus Christ, whose servant he is (4:5). He does not hesitate to remind them of what this service has cost him (6:4–10). At the same time, he knows perfectly well that self-promotion is obnoxious. So he offers such apologies and qualifications as the following: "Not that we are competent of ourselves to claim anything as coming from us; our competence is from God" (3:5). He takes the opportunity to underscore his own weakness and compares himself with a piece of fragile crockery (4:7–12).

Paul rounds out his case with a final apology and a reminder of the devotion he entertains for his addressees, in spite of their having disappointed him: "We have spoken frankly to you Corinthians; our heart is wide open to you. There is no restriction in our affections, but only in yours. In return—I speak as to children—open wide your hearts also" (2 Cor 6:11–13). And, then at this point he takes up a completely different subject, a collection for the Christians in Jerusalem (chs. 8 and 9).

A SECOND APOLOGY
2 CORINTHIANS 10–13

Later in the letter, after this appeal for help for the poverty-stricken fellow Christians in the mother church, we are surprised to find in chapters 10–13 a second defensive speech. It comes genuinely unexpected, popping up abruptly without any connection to the foregoing text. Its tone is quite different besides. The first part of the letter is optimistic, in spite of everything Paul has been saying, but here an obvious pessimism prevails. And the point at issue is new as well. These and other circumstances have led interpreters to wonder whether 2 Corinthians in its present state represents an original unity or whether it consists of several different letters that were later stitched together as one. The simplest answer is perhaps the most plausible: Paul will likely have revised the epistle several times over, possibly after recently receiving bad news from Corinth.

However it may be with the various suggested hypotheses, we can say at least that there is a spirit of discouragement pervading this later portion of the letter. We hear frequently of embarrassment and grief. The tone is violent, and Paul is angry. In his first apology (chs. 1–6) he needed to justify his behavior and uphold his personal integrity, and he does the same again in the beginning of this second one (10:1–18). But what is now at stake is more than his good reputation. It is now nothing less than the authenticity of his apostleship and the consequent authenticity of the understanding of Christ he conveys.

The second apology differs from the first in yet another respect. There he had defended himself against the entire congregation and the evil rumors they were spreading about him. Now he must defend himself against particular opponents, perhaps Jewish Christians. Jewish or otherwise, they are traveling preachers who arrogate to themselves a controling authority, even though they have no warrant for it. Paul sarcastically calls them "super-apostles" (11:5). He insists they are "false apostles, deceitful workers, disguising themselves as apostles of Christ" (11:13).

These opponents he portrays as "commending themselves" (10:12), and therefore Paul feels compelled to fight them on their own ground by doing likewise. From this point on he takes the offensive. In a long section (11:16–13:10), which has been appropriately known as "a fool's speech in his own behalf," he compares himself with them. Here are a few examples of the eloquence fanned into flame by his wrath: "If you are confident that you belong to Christ, . . . so also do we" (10:7). "Let no one think that I am a fool; but if you do, then accept me as a fool, so that I too may boast a little. . . . But whatever anyone dares to boast of—I am speaking as a fool— I also dare to boast of that. Are they Hebrews? So am I. Are they Israelites? So am I. Are they descendants of Abraham? So am I. Are they ministers of Christ? I am talking like a madman—I am a better one: with far greater labors, far more imprisonments, with countless floggings, and often near death" (11:16–23). In support of this claim he adduces an impressive number of dangers and trials: "Five times I have received from the Jews the forty lashes minus one. Three times I was beaten with rods. Once I received a stoning . . . ," and on and on (11:24–29).

But he saves the best for last. To this point he has named his human merits and qualifications. Now he turns to the gifts with which God has endowed him. The Corinthians esteem

and perhaps overvalue extraordinary phenomena such as speaking in tongues and ecstatic experiences. As a rule, Paul is suspicious of this sort of excited behavior (see, e.g., 1 Cor 14:1–23).
Nevertheless he claims that even on this level he is invincible.
Now at last he mentions "the exceptional revelations" he has
been granted (12:7), though he dwells on only one of them.
Here is what he says, and this very text will occupy our attention, point for point, for the remainder of the chapter:

> It is necessary to boast; nothing is to be gained by it, but I will
> go on to visions and revelations of the Lord. I know a person in
> Christ who fourteen years ago was caught up to the third
> heaven—whether in the body or out of the body I do not
> know; God knows. And I know that such a person—whether
> in the body or out of the body I do not know; God knows—
> was caught up into Paradise and heard things that are not to be
> told, that no mortal is permitted to repeat. On behalf of such a
> one I will boast, but on my own behalf I will not boast, except
> of my weaknesses. (2 Cor 12:1–5)

"I KNOW A PERSON IN CHRIST WHO . . ."

This little text is overloaded. Twice it is interrupted with
parenthetical remarks. It is further weighed down with a double
repetition. In place of a free and easy account of himself, as in
the foregoing text, Paul seems suddenly to be speaking of
someone else: "I know a person . . . I know that such a person
. . ." Why does he do this?

The answer is suggested in the closing words of the section: "On behalf of such a one I will boast, but on my own behalf I will not boast, except of my weaknesses" (v. 5). In the
following segment (vv. 6–10) he lists various actual forms of
weakness, among the others something chronic and humiliat-
ing, from which he had prayed three times to be set free, all in
vain. "A thorn in my flesh," he calls it (12:7), but what does he

mean by this? Commentators have puzzled over the phrase and have suggested a range of interpretations. Whether we translate Paul's text more or less literally as "a thorn in his flesh," or with Krister Stendahl render it as "a nuisance which plagues my body," most likely the problem was an illness of some kind. It might have been a depression brought on by malaria picked up in the swamps of Galatia. Indeed, he often talks about his physical infirmity.

Whatever the nature of this weakness may have been, Paul sets "this man" in contrast to himself, as if he were speaking of a doppelgänger, or an alter ego. In his embarrassment, he clearly wishes to distance himself from himself and in this way escape the humiliation he would otherwise be subject to.

"I KNOW A PERSON WHO . . . FOURTEEN YEARS AGO . . ."

Something happened in the past, something quite remarkable in fact, since Paul still remembers it long afterward. He who so often looks to the future now looks to the past. He remembers it as if it were yesterday. It must be a heavily charged memory, one that renders the past perpetually present. Something unusual occurred on a day like any other day, or on a night like any other night. Yet that day, or that night, was different from all others, almost unique.

The fact that we are dealing here with something remarkably unusual can be seen in addition from the contrast between what he says about the things he knows and what he says about the things he does not know. He provides an exact date for the memorable event, but he cannot describe its nature. "Whether in the body or out of the body I do not know; God knows," he says—a bit clumsily for him. And thus he duly informs us of his ignorance. It ought to be enough. Why then does he further burden his story by saying once again, "whether in the body or out of the body I do not know; God knows"?

Why indeed, if not to suggest the mysterious nature of his experience? The linguistic awkwardness reflects his inward confusion. It fits quite well with the story he is telling. Up to this point, he has been burdened by the necessity of defending himself and boasting. Now he is awkward and shy, but for another reason. He has been drawn into something so strange that it has made him a stranger to himself, incapable of knowing even whether his body was with him at the time or not. His usual frame of reference was burst wide open. His present irresolution thus seems to correspond to a sublime exaltation.

Even so, it is also true that alongside Paul's three successive statements of "I do not know," we meet twice his categorical "I know." What is it he knows? What is it he remembers after fourteen years? He remembers that he was caught up to the third heaven.

"HE WAS CAUGHT UP TO THE THIRD HEAVEN"

What is meant here by the verb "to be caught up"? Since the time of Ezekiel it has been a traditional term in Israel for prophetic ecstasies. But what is an ecstasy? This word comes from the Greek expression *ek-stasis,* which refers to being outside oneself. But what does *that* mean? We sometimes say something like "I was beside myself with joy," or "I was beside myself with astonishment." Of course, in such cases we are clearly exaggerating, describing a miniature ecstasy, so to speak. In such cases, the word is much too grand for whatever we are talking about. Yet this common expression can help us understand what a true ecstasy actually is.

A preliminary question of interest here is how a person attains a state of ecstasy. Ethnographers know how people of various cultures throughout the ages have worked themselves into a trance. It can happen through violent dancing, as with dervishes. One can smoke hashish or other stimulants, or chew on hallucinogenic seeds. Or one can resort to repeating magic formulas endlessly. These are just some of the means people have used.

In early Israel, the prophets of Baal worked themselves into a frenzied state by loud cries, wild dances, and other "technical" means, including self-torture. We hear about them in the Book of First Kings: "Then they cried aloud and, as was their custom, they cut themselves with swords and lances until the blood gushed out over them. As midday passed, they raved on until the time of the offering of the oblation, but there was no voice, no answer, and no response" (1 Kgs 18:28–29).

In addition to these deviant Baal worshipers, there were also professional ecstatics among the orthodox adherents of the Lord. In First Samuel, Saul hears these words from Samuel: ". . . as you come to the town [Gibeath-elohim], you will meet a band of prophets coming down from the shrine with harp, tambourine, flute, and lyre playing in front of them; they will be in a prophetic frenzy. Then the spirit of the LORD will possess you, and you will be in a prophetic frenzy along with them and be turned into a different person" (1 Sam 10:5–6).

GOD'S INITIATIVE

Wandering prophets such as these, moving from place to place in groups, must have been relatively unusual. They probably inspired suspicion, leaving people wondering about their sanity.

Certainly, when compared with the great prophets, they were regarded as in a different class. The great prophets did not need to resort to special means to help them attain an ecstatic state. There is, to be sure, one exception to this. Elisha says on one occasion, "Get me a musician!" And when the harpist began to play, the Lord's spirit took hold of Elisha (2 Kgs 3:15). Thus, at least this once, even he made use of a human instrument to inspire a state of inspiration.

But as a rule Elisha and the other genuine prophets stressed instead God's initiative in this, whether they were speaking of their call or of something else. Just a few examples will help us here. At one point Ezekiel writes, "And when he spoke to me, a spirit entered into me and set me on my feet" (Ezek 2:2). In another place he uses a stronger verb: "Then the spirit of the Lord fell upon me" (11:5), like a bird of prey landing on its quarry. In other words we are dealing with a radical interference from outside. It is not merely that God intervenes whenever he likes; the point is that he does so violently, with force, leaving no possibility of resistance.

Much later, Paul implies something similar with the verb he uses in his story: "to be caught up." To "catch up," or to "snatch up," means to jerk something up with violence— something or someone, that is. In certain literary contexts the verb refers to the abduction of a person, often a woman. It is the same thing as a kidnapping, carried out with force; *un rapt,* as the French put it.

In the Latin Vulgate, Paul speaks of being *raptus,* deprived of himself, so to speak. This is why he uses the passive voice, "I *was* caught up." If we are unacquainted with Jewish linguistic conventions, we will not see any particular importance in the use of this form of the verb. But it is highly significant. It is an example of what specialists call a *passivum divinum.* Motivated by respect for God's majesty, the Jews avoided pronouncing his name. Instead they employed various circumlocutions, among others precisely this passive construction. Thus, in our text, the expression "was caught up" means that *God* snatched up Paul. God and God alone took the initiative in what happened. It is for this reason that Paul spoke earlier of "visions and revelations from the Lord" (2 Cor 12:1); that is, they were given to him by the Lord.

Was Paul a mystic, then? In our day the term is ambiguous, even misleading. As soon as modern poets dabble a little in the complexity of human existence, the critics rush to label them as mystics. This is nothing but a lamentable profaning of a term that at one time denoted a special kind of religious phenomenon. Taken in its restricted sense, the designation referred to an unexpected, unrequested gift: the supernatural knowledge God gives regarding his own mysterious nature. It therefore implied a complete passivity on the part of a person who is caught up in a literal moment of grace. No one has any control over it. It is nothing we can prepare ourselves for. This sovereign quality fits exactly with Paul's case. He has never tried to force the experience by his own powers. He has never stirred himself up to a state of ecstasy through religious exercises. He is thus a mystic in the strictest meaning of the word. He fell down in a trance, as it is sometimes put, and we can certainly assume it was a pleasant fall, as into a deep abyss. Or rather, we should say that he fell upward, lifted by the Lord himself. In his own words, he was caught up to the third heaven. But what does *that* mean?

". . . TO THE THIRD HEAVEN . . . INTO PARADISE"

In antiquity the earth was viewed as surrounded by a series of transparent spheres. Judaism believed that divine mysteries were revealed to certain saints as they traveled through those spheres, or heavens, as they were also called. Theories of the number of these heavens changed from time to time. But independently of these variations, the term "heaven" came to refer to the nearness of God in his dwelling place, the dwelling of the Most High, situated far above the surface of the earth. The destination for Paul's journey thus indirectly suggests God's majesty, his transcendence.

Furthermore, the phrase "caught up to the third heaven" implies the thought of happiness and bliss, in the same way as the popular modern saying "to be in seventh heaven." This notion can be seen more clearly in the second expression Paul uses, when he claims that the man he is speaking of was "caught up into Paradise." In his day, paradise was usually regarded as situated precisely in the third heaven, such that the two expressions are synonymous. Thus he was brought into a remote, celestial world of sweetness. But what happened "up there"?

". . . AND I HEARD THINGS . . ."

Paul's account is brief, lacking, for instance, any unnecessary details about the duration of the experience. Instead he points directly to the essential thing, which he mentions last of all: ". . . and I heard things . . ." "Words" (rhēmata) he calls them in Greek, words that no one may speak. He does not say he saw anything, only that he heard something. He did not hear the wordless music of the spheres, only words. For all we can tell, then, it was a visionless experience.

To tell the truth, this was nothing new. In the Jewish tradition reflected in the Old Testament, God's manifestations are far more often auditory than visual, which is hardly remarkable. What the eye sees is concrete, tangible. But it runs the risk of being regarded as mere matter. What is seen is easily reduced to something manageable, something we think we can possess completely. By contrast, what the ear hears is invisible, immaterial. From start to finish it carries an inherent spiritual dignity. It is no accident that music is perceived as exerting a purer, more spiritual effect than a painting does. The fact that in the Old Testament the Lord preferred to speak, rather than to display himself visibly, was clearly a way of preserving his inaccessibility, so that human beings would be less tempted to defile their conception of him. A fully definable God is nothing but a blasphemy.

Still, this take on things can seem a little unsatisfying to us. In another respect, of course, what is heard is subordinate to what is seen. With good reason, sight and hearing are regarded as our two most important senses. And the ability to see is the most highly regarded of all. What is seen is immediately present, even if what we are seeing is a distant star. It is we, we ourselves, who look at it. Only we ourselves, and no one else, can register things through our own sense of sight. Hearing, on the other hand, informs us of something removed from us in time and space. We receive information secondhand from someone (a witness or a storyteller) about something to which we have no immediate access. What Paul was graced with, then, was a report, an account. He learned something indirectly. On the one hand, the vagueness of this can be frustrating for us. But on the other hand, it does say something about the significance of what he was introduced into; it speaks of its remoteness and inaccessibility. And this in itself is uplifting and full of comfort.

By saying that he only heard something, the apostle emphasizes the distance between the heavenly realities and the understanding he gained of them. This divide is evidenced even more by what he adds about the words he did hear: they were words "that are not to be told, that no mortal is permitted to repeat."

"... THINGS THAT ARE NOT TO BE TOLD, THAT NO MORTAL IS PERMITTED TO REPEAT"

Why does Paul use these two verbal expressions, one right after the other? Does he have in mind two separate realities? Most likely they simply reinforce each other, allowing him to express more effectively his radical inability to repeat the words he heard in paradise. Pronouncing them is forbidden not by some sort of divine decree, but because in the very nature of things, doing so is completely impossible. Under no conceivable condition can these heavenly words be translated into earthly language. They defy our ability to conceptualize and consequently they defy our powers of speech. For the realities they describe are too beautiful and far too rich for us.

We sometimes see this even with earthbound realities. Even our greatest poets recognize how difficult, not to say impossible, it can be to clothe our experiences of life in mere words. In the fifth movement of his long prose-poem *Östersjöar* [Eastern Seas] (1974), Tomas Tranströmer writes the following:

> July 30. The bay has become eccentric—today for the first time in years it teems with manatees, they pump themselves along, quiet and indulgent, they all belong to the same shipping firm: AURELIA [the common name for various varieties of manatee], they drift like flowers after a burial at sea, if one takes them from the water all form vanishes from them, as when an indescribable truth is lifted up out of the silence and formulated into a dead gel, they are in fact incapable of translation, they must be left in their own element. (p. 29)

Likewise the words Paul heard in paradise must remain in their proper element. Otherwise they become mere gibberish. Tranströmer continues:

August 2: Something wants to be said but words don't suit it.

Something which cannot be said,

aphasia,

there are no words, but perhaps a touch, a way of . . .

Aphasia, of course. The term appears twice in the poem. Usually it refers to a neuropathological disturbance affecting the speech functions. Something like this afflicted Paul when he was, acoustically as it were, admitted to a divine world beyond all description. He becomes silent. Back on earth again after being transported to rapturous heights, he can say only that he cannot say a thing. We can scarcely improve on this way of expressing the insufficiency of human language in the face of the mystery of God.

It is certainly true that we cannot be confronted with this mystery without risk. Following his encounter with the dazzling vision of the Risen One near Damascus, Paul had been blind for three days, deprived of his powers of sight, seemingly by accident. Now, after the journey to the third heaven, he is in a certain respect unable to speak, incurably so, absolutely mute. He suffers the muteness of wisdom, the silence of the mystics. Fittingly he has lost his ability to talk, at least with respect to the best thing there is for him to talk about. Under such circumstances as these it is understandable that sometimes, perhaps more often than we realize, Paul stands at the very edge of Silence.

Some speakers and writers are interesting because of what they say; others because of the way they say what they say; and still others, like Paul, because of what they do not say.

Chapter 4

A Single Cry Can Be Enough

Galatians 4:6, Romans 8:15

It can sometimes seem difficult to find our way in the theological forest. There is so much we need to read: the New Testament in its entirety, the texts of the great church councils, numerous ecclesiastical documents, more or less official catechisms, not to mention a mountain of writings deriving from various spiritual traditions! It is all too much. Eventually the picture goes blurry. We cannot see the forest for all the trees. Occasionally, then, we long for something more fundamental, something simpler, more unadorned, easier to remember. We want to be able to see the larger picture and to immerse ourselves in what is essential, in what is otherwise common to all Christians. That is, we yearn for something that in utmost simplicity sums up the whole of Christian faith.

Such concentrated formulations do appear here and there in Paul's letters, as for instance when he writes to the Romans, ". . . if you confess with your lips that Jesus is Lord and believe in your heart that God raised him from the dead, you will be saved" (Rom 10:9). There is something central expressed in this summary confession of the faith. When the same apostle listed a number of spiritual gifts for the Corinthians, he wrote, among other things, "no one can say 'Jesus is Lord' except by the Holy Spirit" (1 Cor 12:3). A mere three words: "Jesus is Lord." This single utterance comprises the minimum possible elements needed to form a sentence: subject, verb, and predicate; no adverb, no adjective, nor any other additions. Yet if we read Paul's letters attentively, we may be able to find an even shorter credo.

"AND HE CRIES OUT" GALATIANS 4:6

What motivated Paul, sometime between 54 and 57 C.E., to write to the Galatian believers? He wanted to give a clear answer to a question that was as ticklish for them as it was for the entire early church: Was it possible for gentiles to become Christians without first becoming Jews? That is, was it possible for gentiles to become Christians without submitting to the Mosaic law and, among other things, undergoing circumcision? Paul's answer is an unqualified yes. Without the slightest hesitation he insists that all human beings are welcome in the "Israel of God" (Gal 6:16), and on no other condition than personal consent, that is, faith: "For in Christ Jesus you are all children of God through faith" (3:26). "All," he says, which means gentile Christians as well as Jewish Christians. By this statement he proclaims the theme for the entire following argument, which begins as follows: "As many of you as were baptized into Christ have clothed yourselves with Christ. There is no longer Jew or Greek, there is no longer slave or free, there is no longer male and female; for all of you are one in Christ Jesus. And if you belong to Christ, then you are Abraham's offspring, heirs according to the promise" (3:27–29).

Heirs, he says! His argument involves a long discussion of the Jewish law (2:15–4:11), in which Paul often—and predictably—uses Jewish terminology. He speaks of a "an ordinary human will and testament" (3:15, 17), of "inheritance" (v. 18) and "heirs" (v. 29), of a "custodian" (vv. 24–25), and so on. For the moment, he applies this legal imagery to the Jewish Christians. He counts himself as one of them, and therefore says "we." (When he addresses gentile Christians, as a rule, he uses the second person, "you.") He considers their collective past, which he regards as a temporary arrangement: "Now before faith came, we were imprisoned and guarded under the law until faith would be revealed. Therefore the law was our disciplinarian until Christ came, so that we might be justified by faith. But now that faith has come, we are no longer subject to a disciplinarian" (Gal 3:23–25).

This short text contains several time-indicators: "before faith came . . . until faith would be revealed . . . until Christ came." The perspective is historical. What Paul describes first is a state of affairs like that of a child under supervision, disciplined by a tutor's cane, and thus a form of being underage and without freedom. What he finally says, "but now that faith has come," represents being set free from this disciplinarian, in other words a graduation to majority and independence.

This transition from minority to majority age, in and with the arrival of Christ, is further illustrated in the very next section. There the implied question is whether being a son or a daughter, thus a legal heir, is sufficient justification for having control over an inheritance. The answer of course is no, since it is necessary to wait for the proper time. The perspective continues to be historical, with several temporal markers:

> My point is this: heirs, as long as they are minors, are no better than slaves, though they are the owners of all the property; but they remain under guardians and trustees until the date set by the father. So with us [Jewish Christians]; while we were minors, we were enslaved to the elemental spirits of the world.

> But when the fullness of time had come, God sent his Son,
> born of a woman, born under the law, in order to redeem those
> who were under the law, so that we might receive adoption as
> children. (Gal 4:1–5)

The consciousness of having been brought into this new condition elicits within Christians an inner sense of being adopted as
God's children, which Paul has just mentioned. This now becomes the subject of our meditation.

> And because you are children, God has sent the Spirit of his
> Son into our hearts, crying, "Abba! Father!" So you are no lon-
> ger a slave but a child, and if a child then also an heir, through
> God. (Gal 4:6–7)

Earlier we found a concise sentence that captured the inner
kernel of the Christian faith, namely, "Jesus is Lord." Here,
however, we do not even have a sentence. All we have is a mere
word: "Father!"—"Abba," two unpretentious syllables. Nothing could be briefer.

A CRY

Not only does Paul use this mere, solitary word, but he
also utters it as a cry. He is not thinking of a hesitant mumble
or a shy whisper; he speaks of it as a cry, a shout. It is something
rising irresistibly from deep within us, "in our hearts," as he
puts it. Such an outburst of feeling cannot be feigned; it is
plainer, truer than any chain of words, than any well-consid-
ered discourse.

What Paul has in mind, then, is a spontaneous, even violent, reaction, a kind of primal scream that cannot be held
in once the pressure becomes too great. But what pressure
would that be? When is it that a person cries out? Such a cry
might result from pain, or fear, or horror—from need, that is. A
person also cries out from astonishment, or from being happily

surprised, and this is the case in our text. Behind the outcry Paul speaks of we can infer a shock of joy at something unexpected and enchanting. Apparently then, he is talking of an initial experience. How does a newborn child begin to communicate? It does so through crying, sending out a preverbal signal. In human life, crying precedes speaking, even on the spiritual plane, it seems.

That Paul is actually speaking of an initial encounter, something normally occurring in the beginning of the Christian life, is evident from the literary context. Shortly before claiming that the Spirit cries out within us (Gal 4:6), he reminds the Galatians of their original experience. They "received" the Spirit when they first heard the missionary message and were converted (3:1–2); they "began in the Spirit" (v. 3). He refers to their baptism as well, to the initiatory sacrament through which they put on Christ (v. 27). He is thinking, then, of the very first step in their Christian life, when they were overcome with joy.

WHY ARAMAIC?

As if it were not provocative enough to speak of a cry, Paul specifies this cry's content by means of a foreign term, one he immediately translates: "Abba! Father!" Why does this man who makes such a point of trying to be a Greek to the Greeks (1 Cor 9:19–21) suddenly switch to Aramaic in addressing a Greek-speaking audience? A quick look at some of the rest of the New Testament can provide us the answer.

Mark, the first evangelist, the one who stands chronologically nearest to Christ, sometimes renders expressions of the master in the latter's own language, most likely in order to stand as close to him as possible even in a verbal sense. In one place he has Christ say to Jairus's daughter, *"Talitha cumi!"* which means, "Little girl, get up!" (Mark 5:41). In another

place he has him say to a deaf man, that is, to one whose ears
are "closed," *"Ephphatha!"* meaning, "Be opened" (7:34). Yet a
third time Mark's Christ uses a single heartfelt Aramaic word
as he opens his prayer in Gethsemane: *"Abba!* Father!" (14:36).
Did Jesus begin all his prayers in this intimate way? It is possible. One thing is sure: this one time at least, he broke with the
conventional way of addressing oneself to God. It would never
have occurred to a Jew of the time to speak to God on such a familiar basis. *Abba* means "daddy" or "papa"; it belongs to the
intimate language of childhood.

Christ's model was clearly the minimum requirement
Paul needed for daring to adopt this intimate cry and to en-
courage the Galatians to utter it from their own hearts. And the
fact that the Galatians, without batting an eye, were bold
enough to use it themselves must have been because they believed they were related to Christ. They had good reason to do
so, in fact. They had been taught that they were indeed "the
sons and daughters of God, in Christ Jesus" (Gal 3:26), that
they had "put on Christ" (v. 27), that they "belonged to Christ"
(v. 29). Every one of these verbs points to a level of nearness
bordering on identification, but identification in what sense?

The truth is this: God "sent forth his Son" into the world,
and then he "sent the Spirit of his Son into our hearts" (Gal
4:4, 6). In both instances, Christ is portrayed as the Son par excellence, the Son in a special sense. But Paul insists likewise
that the Galatians too are God's sons and daughters. He insists
on this from the beginning of his argument to the end of it.
His final assertion: "So . . . you are no longer a slave but a
child" (4:7) corresponds exactly with the first one: "you are all

children of God through faith" (3:26). But what does he mean
by this?

There is, of course, a certain difference between Christ
and the Galatians that shows up here and there in the text.
Christ is the Son from the beginning. He was born that way. It
is not so with the Galatians. They have come to their status as
God's children "through faith" (Gal 3:26), that is, through
coming to faith. They have "been made" heirs (4:7), which
implies that they were not heirs from the beginning. They
are presented moreover as having "received adoption as children" (v. 5). The recent Swedish translation *Bibel 2000* puts
it in terms of receiving "the rights of sons." It is not easy
to translate the Greek word *huiothesian,* which Paul alone
uses in the New Testament. Is it enough, with the Swedish
Bible—and many others—to speak of "sonship" without
being more precise? Keeping in mind that the word is a legal
term, Christians from early on, from Jerome to modern trans-
lators in other languages, have rightly used the word "adoption." Though Christ is born a Son, we are, by contrast,
adoptive children. This means, however, that we now par-
ticipate in Christ's own sonship and life. This is so not least
of all with respect to his Spirit, in accordance with a re-
mark we have already noted: "And because you are children,
God has sent the Spirit of his Son into our hearts, crying,
'Abba! Father'" (4:6). It is no one other than the Spirit of
the Son of God himself who cries out in our inmost being. It
is the Son who breathes in us. It is he who shouts for joy
within us over the remarkable fact that we are now at home
with God.

And similarly, once we realize that we have come home,
what Paul said earlier in this same letter is verified: "... it is no
longer I who live, but it is Christ who lives in me" (2:20).

"WHEN WE CRY"
ROMANS 8:15

This initial experience must have been important for Paul, even fundamental for him, since he mentions it again several months later, in the letter to the Romans:

> So then, brothers and sisters, we are debtors, not to "the flesh," to live according to the flesh—for if you live according to the flesh, you will die; but if by the Spirit you put to death the deeds of the body, you will live. For all who are led by the Spirit of God are children of God. For you did not receive a spirit of slavery to fall back into fear, but you have received a spirit of adoption. When we cry, "Abba! Father!" it is that very Spirit bearing witness with our spirit that we are children of God, and if children, then heirs, heirs of God and joint heirs with Christ—if, in fact, we suffer with him so that we may also be glorified with him. (Rom 8:12–17)

In this new letter we recognize several features previously noted in the Galatian letter: the cry "Abba! Father!" and the assurance that we are God's sons and daughters, or God's children, actually God's adoptive children with all the rights and privileges belonging to that status, not least of all the inheritance. In addition, Christ is mentioned here only once, compared with five times in the passage from Galatians. But the Spirit, by contrast, is named five times altogether in this Romans passage, against only once in the Galatians text.

TWO DIFFERENT PERSPECTIVES

The two letters thus have much in common. At the same time, there are several differences between them. The word "slave," to take one example, occurs in both passages, but with somewhat different meanings. In Galatians 4:1–2, the term implies the slave's lack of personal property, a condition comparable with that of a child of the household, so long as that child remains a minor. In Romans, however, reference to servanthood is connected with slavery to sin (Rom 6:12–13; 7:14, 23, 25, and in our text, 8:15), as well as with the fear experienced by a person who unwillingly obeys a dangerous master. There the slave acts so as to escape punishment, rather than on the basis of personal conviction or out of filial devotion.

These and other minor discrepancies arise from the fact that the perspectives of the two letters are somewhat different. As we have seen, the perspective in Galatians is historical. There Paul contrasts two successive periods in the history of salvation: the freedom he speaks of is a freedom from the obsolete Jewish commandments, circumcision and the like. In Romans, the perspective is primarily moral. From the outset, Paul exhorts his readers: "So then, brothers and sisters, we are debtors, not to 'the flesh,' to live according to the flesh—for if you live according to the flesh, you will die; but if by the Spirit you put to death the deeds of the body, you will live" (Rom 8:12–13). The function of the Spirit in this perspective is to help us to "live according to our spirit" (Rom 8:4), that is, according to our "inmost self" (7:22).

In other words, it is a matter of living a spiritual life in the freedom that comes from belonging to God's family, from living under the influence of the Spirit who comes from God. In this way, it is a matter of behaving as children of God (Rom 14). In spite of the differences between the two letters, both teach that the Spirit produces within us a liberating sense of being adopted by God.

"... WITH OUR SPIRIT"

A final difference between Galatians and Romans seems at first sight a little perplexing. According to Galatians 4:6, it is the Spirit who cries out within us; in Romans, however, it is we who cry out (Rom 8:15). Are these two who cry out actually different from each other?

It seems not, for the difference between the two formulations has its explanation in their respective contexts. As we have seen, Paul usually says "we" when he is thinking of Jewish Christians, among whom he counts himself. He does this, for example, in Galatians 4:3–4. There it would have been unfortunate had he said "we," as if he were speaking only of Jewish Christians. The cry is attributed there to all Christians, Jewish or otherwise. He has, additionally, just stressed this universality by insisting that the difference between Jew and Greek is no longer relevant (Gal 3:26–29). A further indication of this universality is that, in one and the same verse (Gal 4:6), he first says "you" (plural), and then speaks of "our" heart, and then in the following verse, he switches back to "you," but now in the singular. Racal specifications such as "Jew," "Greek," "gentile," and so on, no longer mean a thing.

In the parallel text from Romans, to be sure, Paul similarly speaks first in the second person plural (Rom 8:9–11) and then changes to first person plural (vv. 12–27). But here the contrast is not between Jewish and gentile Christians, as is the case in Galatians. In Romans, his use of first person plural "we" stands in opposition to those who continue to live according to their fleshly nature (vv. 4–8)—pagans, in other words. When he writes, "But *you* are not in the flesh [in the sinful nature]" (v. 9), he is referring to the Christians, to all Christians who permit themselves to be led by the Spirit. The difference between "you" and "we" thus loses its significance here. In this way, in one breath and without distinction, Paul can say "we" (v. 12), then "you" (v. 13), and finally "all" (v. 14) as a way of implying "we" and "you" simultaneously. When he consistently employs the first person plural (we, our, us) throughout the following text (vv. 16–27), he is referring to "the saints" (v. 27)—in other words, to all those who believe.

These two facts, the fact that the Spirit cries and the fact that we cry, are actually then one and the same fact. In both cases the Spirit is the driving force. In both cases, everything takes place in our inmost being, in the core of the personality. On the one hand, the Galatians hear that the Spirit of the Son has been sent "into [their] hearts" (Gal 4:6). The Romans, on the other hand, hear that the Spirit of Christ, identical with the Spirit of God (Rom 8:9), dwells within them (v. 11), and that they are led by that Spirit of God (v. 14). Shortly thereafter, Paul expressly mentions the cooperation that takes place between God and human beings: "It is that very Spirit bearing witness with our spirit that we are children of God" (v. 16). Both parties speak the same language, because they are both motivated by the same understanding. We therefore breathe with God's own breath; it is the Spirit in us and with us. Divine wisdom is thus intimately united with human experience.

A SINGLE WORD CAN BE ENOUGH

When Paul wants to summarize the Christian faith in the One whom God sent, he uses an abbreviated confession: "Jesus is Lord" (1 Cor 12:3; Rom 10:9). This confession may well be liturgical, perhaps used in connection with baptism. And when he wants to employ a compressed formulation to epitomize faith in God the Sender, he becomes even more concise, contenting himself with a single word: "Abba! Father!" One word, one cry, one address—the address appears to coincide with the moment a person spiritually reborn utters her first shout of joy. Today we read this outcry perfunctorily, with scarcely any reaction to it. One thing we must freely admit: Paul's talk of a cry of joy strikes us as strange in our own Christian milieu. How many of us have even once uttered a cry of this sort over some

newly discovered religious insight? Has even a single one
of us ever even whispered or murmured anything remotely resembling this kind of exclamation? We might well ask ourselves, where has this shy reserve—not to say total muteness—
come from?

Unsettled by liberal theology, with its antidogmatism and
reductionist minimalism, and simultaneously embarrassed by
extreme ecstatic groups who permit themselves to make arbi-
trary interpretations of the Bible, we can be gripped by mistrust
of the word "experience." Members of churches more con-
cerned with venerating tradition—the orthodox and the Catholic—are sometimes warned against the subjective. The need
for objectivity and right teaching is impressed on them. They
are taught to monitor the correctness of their thinking and to
make sure that it falls in line with traditional doctrine. In and
of itself, this is justifiable, but it is perhaps not entirely without
risk. It would indeed be fatal to our faith if concern for doctrinal purity worked to paralyze us and led us into a frozen
orthodoxy, as if a successful faith were merely a matter of mechanically echoing time-honored formulae without mistakes.
True faith is something better than intellectual conviction.

If we wish to avoid such ideological conformity and sterile
repetition, we should take Paul seriously when he speaks of a
cry, noting that he regards it as something completely natural.
For he does not say, cautiously, "so that we can cry," but "so that
we *do* cry." He assumes in fact that every believer does this,
every single one.

In an earlier letter, when he mentioned being caught up
to the third heaven, he presented it as a unique event occurring
at a particular time and involving a particular individual: "I
knew a man who . . ." (2 Cor 12:2). The experience he speaks of
in Galatians and Romans is something different. Instead of the
singular, he uses the plural: "We are all . . . God's children"
(Gal 3:26); "For all who are led by the Spirit of God are

children of God" (Rom 8:14). The apostle thus reckons with spontaneous responses from all Christians; all of them cry out. He takes for granted an uncontrollable spontaneity. It is as if he had said that it is not forbidden to rely on personal reactions; it is fully permitted to ease up on our self-censuring and to let the Spirit within us do his work unhindered.

Paul's reassurance should thus be enough to calm our fears of subjectivity, to enable us to rehabilitate unforced responses, and to place a higher value on a certain level of immediacy. But clearly it is not enough!

We sense there are likely other factors that paralyze us, including a mistrust of anything elementary, undifferentiated, and therefore difficult to control. We cannot be satisfied with the moment of coming-into-being. We obviously do not appreciate nearly enough the moment of surprise, as if we thought wonder were not the origin of wisdom. Unconsciously influenced by a strange and universal tendency, we allow ourselves to be borne along midstream and to be forever in a rush to analyze, dissect, define, classify, and explain. Surely, whatever precision we win in this analysis is balanced by the depth of understanding we thereby lose.

Volcanologists understand this; they know the amazing swiftness with which a glowing stream of lava cools and hardens. A similar process of petrifying seems to occur on the spiritual level. The original sense of mystery fades quickly and is changed into systematic theology, even—God forbid!—to the point of being degraded into rigid ideology. In Western culture, which still has not freed itself from a shallow rationalism, we are always anxious to do everything in a well-managed way. The danger in this is that both academic theology and popular

Christian living will thereby become pale and anemic. It is impossible without negative consequences to deny the original stage underlying and guaranteeing the continued life of the Spirit.

Perhaps wisdom consists in going upstream, back to the original simplicity, back to the irresistible vitality of the beginning of things. Perhaps in this way our inner life will become, so to speak, more spontaneous, something preliminary to carefully articulated doctrines. When Paul speaks of a kind of preverbal signal, he has no hesitation in using language that precedes language, the childish language we use before adult logic takes over. It is as if he has recommended a theology that precedes theology. It is in any event a fundamental intuition, perhaps a bit of a wild spirituality, preliminary to the dogmatic systematization that often enough results in divisions among the faithful. In one respect, a single word is all he needs: "Abba! Father!"

Chapter 5

From Beastly Bleating to Wordless Sighs

Romans 8:18–27

When Paul speaks of a cry in Romans 8:15, it is not the only time he does so. He is recidivist about it, as a lawyer might say. In the following context (vv. 18–27) he mentions outcries again, three times in fact. We are thus still dealing with preverbal speech, but what sort of preverbal speech? The rich text, even though it is somewhat involved, deserves to be cited in full:

> I consider that the sufferings of this present time are not worth comparing with the glory about to be revealed to us. For the creation waits with eager longing for the revealing of the children of God; for the creation was subjected to futility . . . in hope that the creation itself will be set free from its bondage to decay and will obtain the freedom of the glory of the children of God. We know that the whole creation has been groaning in labor pains until now; and not only the creation, but we ourselves, who have the first fruits of the Spirit, groan inwardly while we wait for adoption, the redemption of our bodies. For

in hope we were saved. Now hope that is seen is not hope. For who hopes for what is seen? But if we hope for what we do not see, we wait for it with patience. Likewise the Spirit helps us in our weakness; for we do not know how to pray as we ought, but that very Spirit intercedes with sighs too deep for words. And God, who searches the heart, knows what is the mind of the Spirit, because the Spirit intercedes for the saints according to the will of God. (Rom 8:18–27)

In this text (vv. 22, 23, 26) as well as in the one preceding it (v. 15), we are dealing with spontaneous outbursts. Paul, using two different Greek verbs, refers to these utterances as cries, groans, and sighs. In verse 15 he uses *krazein,* meaning "to cry out" or "to exclaim." In these three new instances, he uses the verb *stenazein,* which means "to complain" or "to groan." Thus, on the one hand, we have a short cry of joy elicited by a sublime experience, such as learning that God is our father and that we are his adoptive children. On the other hand, we now meet these three drawn-out cries of complaint, uttered in the face of distressing realities. In this new passage the tone is different from what we have in verse 15. It is somber, though it lightens up somewhat toward the end.

In this discourse, Paul proceeds in three stages: he first speaks of the creation (vv. 19–22), then of the believers (vv. 23–25), and finally of the Spirit (vv. 26–27). All three cry out, though in different ways. Let us take them in turn, one by one.

"THE CREATURE'S SIGH"
ROMANS 8:19–22

The preceding section of Romans concerns God's fatherhood and our status as his children. Paul brings that section to a close at 8:17 by claiming that we are "heirs, heirs of God and joint heirs with Christ—if, in fact, we suffer with him so that we may also be glorified with him." He then clarifies his position at the beginning of the next section by employing a similar contrast between a dismal present and a bright future: "I consider that the sufferings of this present time are not worth comparing with the glory about to be revealed to us" (v. 18).

Until now he has been speaking of "us." We expect therefore that he will do the same in the following text, since he introduces it with the word "for" (v. 19), suggesting that he wants to provide an example of what he has just said. However, he apparently changes direction and talks instead of "the creation" (vv. 19, 20, 21), or of "the whole creation," which he describes as experiencing a general frustration (v. 22). But what in fact is it that is subjected to this frustration? Is it the entire universe, or the whole human race, or something else?

Some biblical interpreters understandably take the Greek word *ktisis* (creation) to refer to the soulless, material world. But in Holy Scripture, the entire universe is actually sometimes associated with the fate of humanity, for good or for ill, and this notion is not unfamiliar to Paul. But there are objections that could be lodged against such an understanding of this particular text from Romans. In any case it would not tell the full story. The apostle was no animist. It is difficult to imagine him as viewing stones, trees, and beasts actually experiencing the sensations he mentions here, sensations such as "eager[ly] longing for the revealing of the children of God," or entertaining the hope that they would themselves "obtain the freedom of the glory of the children of God."

So then, should we take the word "creation" to refer to the entire human race? In the Bible generally, and not least in the New Testament, the expression "all creation" is indeed sometimes synonymous with all humanity. Mark's Christ commands his disciples: "Go into all the world and proclaim the good news to the whole creation *[ktisei]*" (Mark 16:15). Similarly, in the Letter to the Colossians, we hear of "the gospel . . . which has been proclaimed to every creature *[ktisei]* under heaven" (Col 1:23). Like the word "world" *(kosmos)* in 2 Corinthians 5:19 and Romans 11:15, then, the term "creation" *(ktisis)* appears to refer to the realm of human beings.

Another reason for identifying "creation" with humanity here is the parallelism between what Paul portrays each as yearning for. On the part of creation is the desire to escape the dominion of futility (Rom 8:20) and to be set free from slavery to decay (v. 21), and on the part of human beings a longing to see God's redemption of their creaturely bodies (v. 23). But redeemed from what? A passage from 2 Corinthians can help us answer that question:

> Even though our outer nature is wasting away, our inner nature is being renewed day by day. For this slight momentary affliction is preparing us for an eternal weight of glory beyond all measure, because we look not at what can be seen but at what cannot be seen; for what can be seen is temporary, but what cannot be seen is eternal. For we know that if the earthly tent we live in is destroyed, we have a building from God, a house not made with hands, eternal in the heavens. For in this [earthly] tent we groan, longing to be clothed with our heavenly dwelling. . . . For while we are still in this tent, we groan under our burden, because we wish not to be unclothed [from our body] but to be further clothed, so that what is mortal may be swallowed up by life. He who has prepared us for this very thing is God, who has given us the Spirit as a guarantee. (2 Cor 4:16–5:5)

What Paul writes to the Corinthians here has much in common with what we have just seen him writing to the Romans. Repeatedly we meet the same features in these two texts. First, the Spirit is presented in 2 Corinthians as a guarantee (2 Cor

5:5), then in Romans as a down payment, a surety (Rom 8:23). Second, we have the contrast between the visible and the invisible, and then between the transitory and the eternal (2 Cor 4:17–18; 5:7; cf. Rom 8:24–25). Third, in both letters Paul contrasts our brief time of suffering with the eternal glory to come (2 Cor 4:17; cf. Rom 8:18). And fourth, on the one hand he speaks in 2 Corinthians of our body, calling it the outer nature, which is wasting away (2 Cor 4:16), or comparing it with an earthly dwelling place, a tent to be torn down (5:1). In Romans, on the other hand, he envisions rescue from decay (Rom 8:21, 23).

Last but not least, both letters use one and the same verb, *stenazein,* which, as we have seen, means "to sigh," "to complain," "to groan" (2 Cor 5:2, 4; Rom 8:22, 23, 26). According to the Corinthian letter, we utter a cry in our "longing" (2 Cor 5:2) or "under our burden" or distress (v. 4). We do this in view of the necessity to "be unclothed" (that is, to die physically), rather than passing directly into glory (that is, to be "further clothed"). Most likely, then, in Romans 8, when Paul mentions creation's hope of being "set free from its bondage to decay," he is thinking of the universality of death (Rom 8:21). Shimmering in the background of this discussion is the hope of resurrection, which Paul has already mentioned in 8:11 and which he will occasionally touch on again, particularly in connection with our coming glorification (vv. 17–30).

Whatever interpretation we may give to these difficult texts, creation is at least to be understood as burdened with something painful. It is not enough that creation longs to be set free from this burden (Rom 8:20b–21), nor that it waits impatiently for something that tarries far too long (v. 19). But it also "groan[s] in labor pains" (v. 22). Its cry is thus a cry of agony, a howl, a beastly yelp, as incapable of restraint as that of a woman in labor.

As an older Swedish translation puts it, "each and every creature sighs and is in anguish . . ." From this rendering Stagnelius gets the title for one of his poems: "The Creature's Sigh." Novelist Sven Delblanc uses the same expression now and then in our day, when he wants to describe his characters' reaction to difficult trials. C. S. Lewis has drawn inspiration from it as well.

"The whole creation has been groaning in labor pains until now." The statement is short, easily read and easily forgotten. Yet it says a great deal. It expresses a timeless, universal complaint, valid over the breadth and width of the entire earth. Nothing less than all humanity finds itself in this hopeless situation. Thousands upon thousands, tens of thousands upon tens of thousands, a great multitude that cannot be reckoned, all peoples, tribes, nations, and languages—all human beings ever born—writhe in the travails of birth and bleat like brute animals. Those who read of this "creaturely sigh" with any sensitivity hear not a harmonious symphony, but a jarring cacophony of whimpering and groaning, of weeping and howling. The phrase "vale of tears" spontaneously comes to mind. We could also speak of an existential angst.

"AND WE OURSELVES . . ."

But Paul has not yet said all there is to say about humanity's lamentable plight. He now adds: "And . . . we ourselves, who have the first fruits of the Spirit, groan inwardly while we wait for adoption, the redemption of our bodies" (Rom 8:23). By saying "and we ourselves"—that is, we Christians—he appears to be introducing a new group of beings, different from those covered by the term "creation." But this is far from certain. In the first place, no one can logically stand outside of, or separate from, "all creation," that is, beyond what is universally all-inclusive. The one cannot be added to the other. Moreover, the section on creation (vv. 19, 21) is framed by *two* passages that focus on "us" (vv. 12–18, and 22–27), one of which we have already met.

In the second place, what Christians yearn for—that the glory of Christ will be revealed and become their own (Rom 8:18)—is identical with what the creation impatiently awaits, namely, "the revealing of the children of God" (v. 19). The verb "reveal" occurs in both verses. Likewise, what the Christians are said to be waiting for, namely, "adoption [as God's children], the redemption of [their] bodies" (v. 23), exactly corresponds to the hope entertained by creation. What creation hopes for is that it "will be set free from its bondage to decay and will obtain the freedom of the glory of the children of God" (v. 21). In both these verses, we meet again with matching occurrences of one and the same verb: "be set free."

From this we can conclude that the believers are to be included as an integral part of the entity known as creation. But how are they then to be distinguished from the rest of humanity?

The object of their anticipation can be a bit confusing. On the one hand, we hear them described as still waiting for God to make them his sons and daughters (Rom 8:23). On the other hand, in the preceding text Paul has clearly and unambiguously insisted that they are actually God's children already (*huioi,* v. 14; *tekna,* v. 16). But if that is the case, what can he possibly mean by saying that they are still waiting for it?

Of course, what remains unfulfilled for them, thus calling forth their sense of frustration, must be the full manifestation of their divine adoption, that is, a complete unveiling of the glory which properly belongs to God's children (Rom 8:21). The word "glory" is indeed a keyword in this entire context (vv. 17, 18, 21, 30). But it refers to a coming reality. Christians are constantly faced with the fact that the ultimate manifestation of their adoption may be delayed a long while yet. Things are only in the beginning stages, and it may indeed be some time yet before believers will "be conformed to the image of [God's] Son" (v. 29), that is, before they will partake of the glorification equivalent to final salvation (v. 24). And it is precisely this period of delay that provokes these feelings of frustration.

But Paul directs his gaze toward the future, which in his view is already here. Several verbs in this section are in the future tense (Rom 8:18, 19, 21, 23), and the concept of "hope" plays an important role in the context. But this particular hope represents something more than a vague wish. Creation, says Paul, waits with "eagerness" (v. 19); believers wait "with patience" (v. 25). And it is exactly in this regard that they are different from the rest of the human race. Their hope is founded on the witness of the Spirit (v. 16). For the time being, of course, they have the Spirit as "the first fruits" (v. 23), as a kind of collateral. But the Spirit is all they need in order to be able to regard the future as completely assured.

"LIKEWISE THE SPIRIT HELPS US IN OUR WEAKNESS" ROMANS 8:26–27

How does Paul bring this discussion of humanity's precarious situation to a conclusion? He has depicted creation as waiting impatiently and crying out as if in the pains of labor (Rom 8:19–22). He has characterized the faithful as patiently waiting and uttering a cry inspired by a more specific hope (vv. 23–25). Now for a third and final time, he again mentions a cry, one uttered this time by him who intervenes in our stead. Paul writes: "Likewise the Spirit helps us in our weakness; for we do not know how to pray as we ought, but that very Spirit intercedes with sighs too deep for words. And God, who searches the heart, knows what is the mind of the Spirit, because the Spirit intercedes for the saints according to the will of God" (Rom 8:26–27).

To this point, Paul has spoken of two distinct ways in which the Spirit involves himself in the affairs of our heart. He first of all enables us to understand that God is our father and that we are his adopted children (Rom 8:15–16). On the basis of this conviction the Spirit gives us hope, hope that our adoptive state will one day be revealed in all of its implied consequences (v. 23). And second, Paul now portrays this same Spirit as helping us to pray.

Do we really need an external help like this? Oh, yes! says Paul, "for we do not know how to pray as we ought" (Rom 8:26b). He argues this from our own human experience, from our hesitation, from what he refers to as "our weakness." We know neither *what* we should pray for (*ti* in Greek), nor *how* we should pray for it *(katho dei)*. We would find ourselves in a hopeless situation if we were left to our own resources. But another person rushes to our side, a mediator, an intercessor, none other than God's own Spirit, who is the only one who can really pray "according to the will of God" (v. 27).

In one sense, he does this in our place; Paul depicts the Spirit as making his appeals on our behalf. Yet the Spirit does not intercede within us as if he were an unfamiliar guest, or as if our inner person were merely a passive vessel. For God actually "searches the heart, [and] knows what is the mind of the Spirit" (Rom 8:27a). Just a few lines earlier, as we have seen, Paul writes that "When we cry, 'Abba! Father!' it is that very

Spirit bearing witness with our spirit that we are children of God" (8:15–16), a statement that closely resembles what we find in Galatians. There we read: "God has sent the Spirit of his Son into our hearts, crying, 'Abba! Father!' " (Gal 4:6). The fact that the same cry is said to be uttered in the one instance by us, and in the other by the Spirit within us, witnesses to a harmonious accord: the Spirit within us and we ourselves cry out in unity.

LEAVING EVERYTHING OPEN

Paul realizes that we know neither what to pray for nor how to pray for it. This is largely true, of course, perhaps most of the time. However, we also know too much. We want this and we want that; we want anything for which we think we are in great need. This approach to prayer can be defended in certain situations, to judge by what we read in the gospels. Some people there loudly call out their petitions. They boldly persist, in spite of protests from the surrounding crowd. "Jesus, Son of David, have mercy on me! . . . let me see again," cries the blind man in Jericho (Luke 18:38, 41). Or they make a desperate appeal, like the father of the epileptic boy: "I believe; help my unbelief" (Mark 9:24). Who would reproach them for their attempt to influence, even force, a benefactor? Need obeys no law. These people rightly pay no attention to consequences. They do not hesitate to storm even the gates of heaven. The fact that their petitions are finally heard means that their outspokenness has been deemed acceptable.

Others demonstrate more restraint. They do not cry out. They make no request, at least they make none directly. They only make the situation known, in all modesty. This is what the tactful Mary did at Cana, when she whispered to Jesus, "They have no wine" (John 2:3), or what the sisters Martha and Mary of Bethany did when they sent word to

Jesus, "Lord, he whom you love is ill" (John 11:3). These prayers are scarcely prayers at all; they are merely implied appeals, marked by a confidence in the addressee's abilities and by a reverential deference to his personal integrity. In these cases he is able to draw his own practical conclusions and to act according to his own wisdom. The initiative is left entirely in his hands.

Till now Paul has been speaking of prayers offered in an articulate, though increasingly discrete way. Most discrete of all is the Spirit's prayer in Romans 8. The noteworthy thing there is that the Spirit does not rescue us by prompting us to say all the right words, words that then must be faithfully repeated. Rather, he himself prays within us "with sighs too deep for words." He only inspires our longing and leads us to sigh, to groan, as we wait for something. But this something is not mentioned specifically. It is never clearly said "what the mind of the Spirit" is. The only thing Paul does say is that the Spirit makes his appeals "according to the will of God" (v. 27).

Paul's discretion can seem troublesome for those who all too frequently think they know exactly what they need. In actual fact, however, Paul's way of viewing things can be beneficial and liberating for believers. Their overconfidence, even if they are unaware of it, can block the Spirit in such a way that he has no possibility of interceding on his own terms. Thus Paul indirectly urges his readers that they refrain at least occasionally from specifying their demands, and that they content themselves merely with "sighs too deep for words." He wants them to leave the matter open. The important thing is only to sigh and to wait. The Spirit knows best where he will blow, and when, and how; the risk in this is that our comfortable expectations will be disturbed by the Spirit's unpredictability. Yet this complete openness to him is possibly one of the best of all forms of prayer.

Chapter 6

On to a Final Silence

Romans 11:33–36

Compared with other letters, the one Paul addressed to the Romans lacks drama. The tone is quiet, objective, and controlled. For this reason, rightly or wrongly, individual interpreters have read the letter as a theological tractate, a literary genre dependent on impersonal objectivity. Yet even here the apostle mentions several times, one after another, shouts, cries of need, and groanings. But he does so in a purely descriptive way, as if he were observing them only from without. Even when he writes, "we ourselves . . . groan" (Rom 8:22–23), he is speaking collectively, and the way he says it implies a certain distance.

We do note, however, that further on in the letter he does speak in his own name and there utters a lofty exclamation, to which we will presently to return: "O the depth of the riches and wisdom and knowledge of God!" (Rom 11:33). But in order to understand a text like this, it is wise to begin by observing its context, its literary coherence. In other words, we will succeed only by first observing the letter's arrangement and its structure.

Romans clearly falls into two main divisions: a theoretical one and a practical one. The didactic part, covered in chapters 1–11, is devoted to teaching, and the moralistic part, covered in chapters 12–15, is devoted to admonition. The apostle's concrete advice, which comes in the second half, follows naturally from his grand vision, depicted in the first half. After the teaching statements, formulated with verbs in the indicative mood, come the admonitions, formulated with verbs in the imperative mood. It is as if the apostle says, "Become what you are!"

The teaching half itself falls into two parts. First comes an unusually well-designed section, chapters 1–8, constituting the most cohesively constructed stretch of text in all the Pauline letters. There, if anywhere, Paul shows that he knows how to round off a segment with a striking final comment. In fact, a total of six times he concludes successive stages of his discussion by mentioning the role played by the man he emphatically calls "Jesus Christ, our Lord" (Rom 4:24; 5:11, 21; 6:23; 7:25; 8:39). He refers to him in an especially energetic way at the end of very last paragraph (8:38–39). What does this paragraph look like?

A DOUBLE CHANGE OF REGISTER
ROMANS 8:28–39 AND 11:33–36

To this point, Paul has shown himself to be a practiced dialectician. From the beginning of the epistle he has given proof of a formidable skill in logic, even if he sometimes becomes tedious about it. The letter swarms with strict argumentation, marked by a mass of logical signals such as "for," "therefore," and "since." But toward the end of this first major section he changes his style. Up to this point he has reasoned out his case, if not exactly coolly, then at least in a controlled, almost impersonal way. Now though he begins to wax lyrical, writing with heartfelt fervency. This gradual change in style is characterized first of all by rhythmic repetitions: The people whom God "foreknew he also predestined to be conformed to the image of his Son. . . . And those whom he predestined he also called; and those whom he called he also justified; and those whom he justified he also glorified" (Rom 8:29–30).

The change is further marked by a series of rhetorical questions: "What then are we to say about these things? If God is for us, who is against us? . . . Who will bring any charge against God's elect? . . . Who will separate us from the love of Christ?" (8:31–35). Lastly, as an answer to these defiant questions, comes a series of "neither/nor" statements, which by their dense concentration convey the impression of a joyful assurance of victory:

> [I]n all these things we are more than conquerors through him who loved us. For I am convinced that neither death, nor life, nor angels, nor rulers, nor things present, nor things to come, nor powers, nor height, nor depth, nor anything else in all creation, will be able to separate us from the love of God in Christ Jesus our Lord. (Rom 8:37–39)

At the end of the letter's first main doctrinal section, (chs. 1–8), the emotional intensity gradually rises to a climax.

By the time he gets to this point, Paul has said all he has to say regarding his main topic, God's universal salvation. Yet he takes it up again in a kind of appendix, as an explanation or an illustration of the subject applied to the special case of Israel's final destiny (chs. 9–11). This section, too, like the preceding one, ends in something distinct from the rest in terms of style. Here as well, in the teaching portion's second climax, Paul slides into a vibrato. Following a final statement summarizing everything he has said so far ("For God has imprisoned all in disobedience so that he may be merciful to all" [Rom 11:32]), there now comes a lyrical conclusion, which in its entirety runs like this:

> O the depth of the riches and wisdom and knowledge of God!
> How unsearchable are his judgments and how inscrutable his
> ways! For who has known the mind of the Lord? Or who has
> been his counselor? Or who has given a gift to him, to receive a
> gift in return? For from him and through him and to him are
> all things. To him be the glory forever. Amen. (Rom 11:33–36)

This is how the didactic half of Paul's letter ends, and it is now
these very verses that demand our attention.

A RADICAL CAPITULATION

In the letter's first main part we mount up twice to a kind
of culmination. In order to focus on the peculiar nature of the
second of these, it can be useful to compare it with the earlier
one and take note of a number of dissimilarities between them.
In the first place, this second text is shorter than the first one,
almost like silence in comparison. In the second place, the
change in register, or style, while taking place somewhat gradually in chapter 8, occurs rather suddenly in chapter 11. Paul
has argued purposefully in this latter section, presenting his
thesis more or less objectively. But now he comes to a dead stop.
He is done with arguments, and we encounter here an abrupt
shift in style and intent.

Third, the rhetorical questions we find in both texts are of
different kinds. To those in chapter 8, which have largely to do
with whether anything can ever separate us from the love of
Christ, Paul answers with a firm "Nothing!" (Rom 8:37).
These questions are aimed at clarifying a long discussion regarding God's unexpected love for humanity, manifested in
Christ. They illustrate what Paul was thoroughly convinced
of, namely that God is for us (8:31). But the rhetorical questions he raises in chapter 11—"Who has known the mind of
the Lord?"—have an opposite purpose: they demonstrate the

letter-writer's total inability to answer them. In chapter 8, he says that he is "certain" that nothing can resist God's achievement of salvation (8:38). His "neither/nor" statements make this very clear. But in chapter 11, he affirms his own ignorance, and in fact everyone's, too. No one is in a position to understand what has motivated the divine deliverance. It is precisely our ability to conceptualize that is called into question here—denied, in fact. It is a matter of a radical capitulation.

To this point he has been teaching. He has kept his subject under control, like the learned and skillful instructor he is. But now for a moment he comes down from his lectern, virtually falling out of it, in fact! He lets go of his scholarly control and falls speechless, though not literally speechless; he does continue writing after all, even eloquently. But he continues writing only in order to claim that speech now fails him. He finds he has nothing worthy to say about this reality that overwhelms him.

A EUPHORIC CAPITULATION

In some situations, being confronted with something we cannot possibly understand leaves us paralyzed. Failure of this sort can bring about weary sadness or dispirited resignation. If the game is lost before we even begin to play, what good is there in making any effort to understand it?

Here, however, we have nothing of the kind. Paul's capitulation at this point is utterly different from any kind of depression. On the contrary, this entire final paragraph is filled with wonder and admiration. It breathes with delight and surprise. Paul is dumbstruck with trembling humility in the face of something that surpasses his comprehension, but something that simultaneously fascinates him with its immeasurable depth and richness. His pounding heart takes over where his brain is overmatched. We can rightfully speak of a euphoric capitulation. The very style of his writing betrays his joyful frame of mind. He virtually gives us a song, a piece of poetry. It begins with two ecstatic cries (Rom 11:33) and continues with three rhetorical questions expressing amazed rejoicing (vv. 34–35).

This "song" ends by answering Paul's third question: "Who has given a gift to [God], to receive a gift in return?" The answer is implied: No one! The reason: "For from him and through him and to him are all things" (Rom 11:36a). This formula is almost liturgical. But the final verse is definitely so: "To him be the glory forever. Amen!" (v. 36b). The song is a song of praise. Just as poetry is more expressive than prose and singing more than recitation, an offer of praise to God says more than any theological speculation can ever do, no matter how profound. We can always praise what we cannot understand. A song of praise is both a recognition of inability and an expression of reverence for what cannot be comprehended, but can be only felt.

Paul's final paragraph in its entirety is thus a hymn to divine wisdom, a piece of music hinting at what cannot be articulated in abstract concepts. And that is as it should be. It is how everything should end. Any theology that does not result in singing God's praise is simply bad theology.

Part Three

Beyond Words by Means of Words

Chapter 7

An Unveiled Secret

Romans 16:25–27

In spite of his talkative nature, Paul has a keen instinct for the inexpressible. He stands in speechless amazement before the depth and richness of divine wisdom. In order to refer to this reality, one that defies our ability to grasp it, he uses the Greek word, *mystērion,* from which we get our word "mystery." In fact, he uses this term more often than any other New Testament writer does. What do we understand him to mean by it?

In common use, the term leads us to think of something incomprehensible. In the same way, the adjective "mystical" makes us think of something strange, shrouded in the mist. This sort of meaning is not all that foreign to Paul. When he criticizes the Corinthians' childish fascination with sensational manifestations of the Spirit, including ecstatically speaking in tongues, he writes: "For those who speak in a tongue do not speak to other people but to God; for nobody understands them, since they are speaking mysteries in [a spiritual rapture]" (1 Cor 14:2). And a few verses later he says to anyone who speaks like this: "the outsider [the uninitiated] does not know what you are saying" (v. 16).

Many people associate the notion of "mystery" with the unintelligible, with what is dark and puzzling. Even in our day of unimaginative rationalism, they are drawn *a contrario* to the mysterious: the Bermuda triangle, UFOs, the secrets of the pyramids, the lost treasure of the Knights Templar, and other historical enigmas. Unexplained phenomena tickle their need for excitement.

Likewise, not a few pious Christians are especially intrigued with the darker passages in the Bible. In fact, they value the Bible precisely because it *is* dark. The more impenetrable a text, the better. This is why they love to read the prophet Daniel and to brood over what he must have meant by the king who comes to afflict the faithful "for a time, two times, and half a time" (Dan 7:25). This formula is echoed in John's Apocalypse (12:14), alongside other chronological indicators, such as "forty-two months" (11:2) and "one thousand two hundred sixty days" (11:3; 12:6). Obscure passages like these capture the attention of romantic believers and sometimes inspire them to devote themselves to wild speculations about the date of the end of time.

Thus a number of believers and nonbelievers have in common this attraction to the occult, as if another world existed behind reality. Few modern authors have mocked this false sense of the mysterious with such mischievous delight as Umberto Eco does in his novel *Foucault's Pendulum*. How does Paul view the subject?

A SECRET KEPT HIDDEN AND THEN UNVEILED

Among the letters rightly or wrongly attributed to Paul, the one addressed to the Ephesian church is the richest of all in its treatment of mystery, especially in Ephesians 3:1–13. But the word *mystērion* itself occurs most often in 1 Corinthians. There Paul says he proclaims "the mystery of God" (1 Cor 2:1) and "God's wisdom, secret and hidden" (v. 7), that is, *both* secret *and* hidden. He does not expressly say that it was later revealed. But he must surely take that for granted, since he insists that he now proclaims it. While he does not specify here the time of this presumed unveiling, he does make it plain and clear in a later letter:

> Now to God who is able to strengthen you according to my gospel and the proclamation of Jesus Christ, according to the revelation of the mystery *[mystērion]* that was kept secret for long ages but is now disclosed, and through the prophetic writings is made known to all the Gentiles, according to the command of the eternal God, to bring about the obedience of faith—to the only wise God, through Jesus Christ, to whom be the glory forever! Amen. (Rom 16:25–27)

This solemn eulogy, rounding out the present state of the letter to the Romans, is rather overloaded. Nevertheless its basic idea is clear. Two periods in the history of humanity are contrasted here. On the one hand Paul speaks of "long ages" gone by; on the other hand he speaks of a new "now." What marks the transition from the one period to the other is that a secret, long kept hidden, has now been disclosed.

A similar division in time appears in two later letters, which (all things considered) are not written by Paul himself, though they probably come from his staff, or from a "Pauline school." What does the author of Colossians say about the word of God? He calls it "the mystery that has been hidden throughout the ages and generations but has now been revealed to his saints" (Col 1:26). The writer of Ephesians builds partly on the Letter to the Colossians. So it is not unexpected that when speaking of "the mystery hidden for ages in God"

(Eph 3:9), he in turn writes, "In former generations this mystery was not made known to humankind, as it has now been revealed . . ." (v. 5).

To judge from the contrast that occurs in each and every one of these three texts, the word *mystērion* has a distinct meaning in them. It refers to something that was first kept secret and then later was revealed, and revealed at a particular point in time. The question is, when? Can this event be dated?

". . . THE FULLNESS OF TIME" EPHESIANS 1:10

Our three epistles were written between 57 C.E. and somewhere in the 60s. The references to "now" in them must signify something having taken place at an earlier time. But can we be more precise about it?

Let us go back to the oldest of them: the letter to the Romans. There Paul states several times that something important has recently occurred. After a rather dark portrayal of humanity's failure to measure up to God's standards, even from the beginning of time (Rom 1:18–3:20), he mentions emphatically a literally epoch-making event that stunningly contrasts with the foregoing situation. "But now, apart from law, the righteousness of God has been disclosed . . ." (Rom 3:21). Shortly thereafter he adds that God put Christ forward "as a sacrifice of atonement by his blood, effective through faith. He did this to show his righteousness, because in his divine forbearance he had passed over the sins previously committed; it was to prove at the present time that he himself is righteous" (vv. 25–26). Already here, in chapter 3, two epochs stand in opposition: after a "previously" and a "time of forbearance" we hear of the "present time," when God mercifully intervened in Christ.

Christ's achievement is mentioned again in chapter 5 in order to mark a decisive change in human history: "For while we were still weak, at the right time Christ died for the ungodly" (Rom 5:6). This must certainly mean the messianic time, the one mentioned by John the Baptist (Mark 1:15: "The time is fulfilled, and the kingdom of God has come near") and ushered in by Jesus. Somewhat later, the author of the letter to the Hebrews will write: "Long ago God spoke to our ancestors in many and various ways by the prophets, but in these last days he has spoken to us by a Son, whom he appointed heir of all things, through whom he also created the worlds" (Heb 1:1–2). Thus the antithetical pair "earlier/now" appears frequently in the New Testament in order to set the time before Christ and the time after Christ in opposition. What we want to know is what was revealed at the beginning of our era. But first we should ask who is it who reveals this secret.

In three of the letters cited above, the verbs "disclose," "reveal," and "make known" appear in the passive voice (Rom 16:25–26; Col 1:26; and Eph 3:3, 5). Here we recognize once again what scholars call a divine passive, common among Jews as a way to speak of God without using his name. Thus, when Paul writes about "the mystery that was kept secret for long ages" (Rom 16:25), he apparently means that God has kept it secret. When he continues, "but [it] is now disclosed" (v. 26a), he means, similarly, that God has disclosed it.

In addition, when he immediately adds that the secret "is made known . . . according to the command of the eternal God" (Rom 16:26b), Paul clearly asserts that God, and no other, first freely kept the secret to himself and only later, again of his own free will, let it be made known. This raises the question: Who is granted the privilege of this initiation into the secrets of God?

"... TO HIS HOLY APOSTLES AND PROPHETS" EPHESIANS 3:5

At the end of Romans, Paul appears to reckon with two stages in this initiation, and with two successive addressees: the secret is first "disclosed" (Rom 16:25) and then "made known" to all nations (v. 26). Who received that first disclosure, before the secret was made more widely available to a broader circle of receptors?

In his first letter to the Corinthians, Paul speaks of both himself (1 Cor 2:1, 4) and of the apostles as mediators of God's mysterious wisdom (beginning at v. 6 he shifts from "I" to "we"). Likewise the author of Ephesians regards himself as belonging to the initiated: "the mystery was made known to me by revelation" (Eph 3:3). Regardless of whether Paul himself is the writer here or whether he communicates through a co-worker, the words evoke the story of the call of the apostle to the gentiles as he was on his way to Damascus. There, precisely through a revelation, he was sent out to all peoples, as both Galatians (1:15–16) and Acts (26:16–17) agree in testifying. In the same letter to Ephesus, in the very same passage in fact, we hear that the secret, long kept under wraps, "has now been revealed to his holy apostles and prophets by the Spirit" (Eph 3:5).

But who exactly is meant here by "apostles and prophets"? Presumably they are identical. If that is the case, then the apostles are viewed as prophets because something has been disclosed to them "by revelation" (3:3), "by the Spirit" (v. 5). Already in 1 Corinthians Paul himself claims that God has revealed his secret "through the Spirit" (1 Cor 2:10). In the same way as with the Old Testament prophets, then, the Christian apostles have been blessed with prophetic gifts of the sort mentioned later in the same letter, where they are portrayed as enabling a person "to understand all mysteries" (13:2).

". . . TO HIS SAINTS"
COLOSSIANS 1:26

The divine mystery is not disclosed to a small number of people only, as if to an elite group. The intention is that it will be spread abroad, that it will be "proclaimed." This latter verb occurs no fewer than five times in the section where Paul tells the Corinthians about the mystery (1 Cor 2:1, 4, 6, 7, 9). Later in his second letter to Corinth, he writes: "But thanks be to God, who . . . through us spreads in every place the fragrance that comes from knowing [Christ]" (2 Cor 2:14). "In every place," he says. At the end of the letter to the Romans, he says that the secret has been made known "to all the Gentiles . . . to bring about the obedience of faith" (Rom 16:26).

Also in Colossians, God's revelation and its widespread proclamation are associated with each other. First the writer speaks of "the gospel . . . which has been proclaimed to every creature under heaven" (Col 1:23). Then he says that this gospel's content is a secret about Christ, which has been revealed "to [God's] saints" (that is, to all the believers, v. 26) and which especially concerns the "Gentiles" (v. 27). Finally he says: "It is he whom we proclaim, warning everyone and teaching everyone in all wisdom, so that we may present everyone mature in Christ" (v. 28). The adjective "all/every" is repeated three times here. These same people, far beyond the borders of Judaism, are the subject likewise in Ephesians, where the author claims he has received grace "to bring to the Gentiles the news of the boundless riches of Christ, and to make everyone see what is the plan of the mystery hidden for ages in God" (Eph 3:8–9).

The various designations for those who receive the proclamation—"all," "all nations," "all creatures," "all people," even "the gentiles"—speaks very clearly. There is nothing esoteric about the Christian message. It is not to be kept back by a small circle of initiates. Such elitism is completely foreign to Paul and his school.

". . . THROUGH THE PROPHETIC WRITINGS" ROMANS 16:26

How was it possible for the apostles to interpret this message in such a way that their hearers or readers could understand it? For one thing, they were able to place in historical perspective what had happened "in their own day" (Rom 3:26). What had only recently happened was, of course, something new, but it had been prepared for and hinted at from much earlier times.

Paul loves to cite the Old Testament, not least when he addresses Jewish Christians. He is careful to point out the continuity in God's saving achievement. The first time he takes up the matter of the divine mystery, he borrows words from the prophet Isaiah (1 Cor 2:9; Isa 64:4). Later, at the opening of Romans, he speaks of the gospel, "which he promised beforehand through his prophets in the holy scriptures" (Rom 1:2). This event that has recently come to pass is thus the fulfillment of ancient promises. Further on in Romans, Paul affirms that "the Jews were entrusted with the oracles of God" (3:2), implying that God had spoken earlier. And in verse 21, Paul again insists that "the righteousness of God has been disclosed, and is attested by the law and the prophets."

It is not easy to determine what Old Testament texts he has in mind here. But one thing we can say: the word *mystērion* itself is a keyword for the prophet Daniel. There, among other things, we hear that the Lord gives the wise their wisdom and reveals to them the deep and hidden things (Dan 2:21–23, 28–30, 47). Paul apparently got his vocabulary from this source. With support from exactly such texts as these, he can make his gospel clear, as he says in Romans when he speaks of a mystery "now disclosed, and through the prophetic writings . . . made known to all the Gentiles, according to the command of the eternal God" (Rom 16:26). The assumption here is that the New Testament brings to the light of day what the Old Testament had already borne witness to and promised, even if only in an obscure way.

THE CONTENT OF THE SECRET DISCLOSED

So what is it, then, that has been kept secret for so long? What has God finally unveiled? What is it that the apostles proclaim "with the help of the prophetic writings"?

In one letter after another we hear of "God's purpose" (Rom 8:28), of his free election (9:11), or of his "will" in the sense of his purposes for humanity (Col 1:9). Nowhere, however, is his free election so intimately connected with the divine mystery as in the Letter to the Ephesians. In chapter 1 the author speaks of "the good pleasure of his will" (Eph 1:5), of "his counsel and will" (v. 11). He does so precisely in connection with what has recently been revealed: "[God] has made known to us the mystery of his will, according to his good pleasure that he set forth in Christ" (v. 9). But the connection is made most closely in chapter 3. In the same breath as he mentions "God's purpose" (the NRSV puts it as "the commission"), the writer also speaks of the grace he has received "to make everyone see what is the plan of the mystery hidden for ages in God" (v. 9). And just two verses later we hear of God's "eternal purpose" for the world (v. 11).

And what is this purpose? It is mentioned in the same paragraph where, speaking of "the mystery of Christ" (Eph 3:4), the author writes: "the Gentiles have become fellow heirs, members of the same body, and sharers [with us Jews] in the promise in Christ Jesus through the gospel" (v. 6). Additionally, the Ephesian Christians read that they who were previously heathens have heard the message of "the unsearchable riches of Christ" (v. 8). And as we have seen, the entire doctrinal section of Romans focuses on this universality of salvation.

What stands at the center of the divine secret is thus God's plan; it is actually a plan for salvation, and one that concerns all human beings without exception. Even those who once stood beyond the pale, from a Jewish perspective at any rate, now have access to God's gifts. This is as plain as day. It does not require any special sharp-wittedness to understand that God's act of rescue is offered to all humanity, absolutely all, without regard to race, gender, or social status. This much is crystal clear.

At least this was the case for the first gentile Christians: crystal clear and exhilarating all at once. No one could have predicted that gentiles would ever have had a part in the privileges of Jewish Christendom. We ourselves may read this without blinking and with relative indifference. The reason for this is that we who are *goyim*—that is, non-Jews—forget that we are the descendants of those gentiles. The reason may also be that we have simply read this text far too often. Any form of familiarity can become fatal. Blind as we are from being accustomed to what we know all too well, we easily undervalue it. In this way, what is well known becomes what is badly known.

This can be the case with the Greek word that sums up the revealed secret: *euangelion*. As is widely recognized, this term means "glad tidings" or "good news." But this news, repeated in season and out for nearly two thousand years, has ceased to be news. It has long since become flat and stale. It has lost its novelty and thus its disturbing effect. How can we reinfuse it with its original power to provoke? It can be done only by distancing ourselves from it, or (more simply) by removing from us what has been so close to us that it makes us nearsighted. To do this requires swimming against the current, back to the source, back to frame of mind characterizing those who heard the news the first time. It means going back to the ancient gentiles, since in one respect, they were the privileged receivers of God's universal deliverance.

At one point in the Acts of the Apostles, Luke reports how Paul and Barnabas spoke with great success in the synagogue of Pisidian Antioch:

> But when the Jews saw the crowds, they were filled with jealousy; and blaspheming, they contradicted what was spoken by Paul. Then both Paul and Barnabas spoke out boldly, saying, "It was necessary that the word of God should be spoken first to you. Since you reject it and judge yourselves to be unworthy of eternal life, we are now turning to the Gentiles. For so the Lord has commanded us, saying, 'I have set you to be a light for the Gentiles, so that you may bring salvation to the ends of the earth.'" [Isa 49:6] When the Gentiles heard this, they were glad and praised the word of the Lord; and as many as had been destined for eternal life became believers. (Acts 13:45–48)

The universal applicability of the gospel was by no means understood from the beginning; it explains the outsiders' joy in this passage.

Two chapters later, Luke takes up the Jerusalem Council, at which the apostles debated the conditions necessary for a non-Jew to be admitted to the New Israel. At the end of the meeting, they determined not to lay upon the gentile believers any unnecessary Mosaic commandments. They sent an official letter to the inhabitants of Syrian Antioch confirming this decision. Luke reports that when the Christians at Antioch read the letter, "they rejoiced at the exhortation" (Acts 15:31). For them, this was truly good news, something to be surprised at and to celebrate. We could wish that later generations would likewise experience the same shock of surprise at this communication. No spiritual life can be kept alive without a continually renewed sense of wonder. Wonder in fact is the beginning of wisdom. It is also its continuation and its fulfillment, if we do not wish to die prematurely.

REVEALED IN PLAIN SPEECH

In spite of any difficulty we later Christians may have in actually appreciating the revolutionary side of the long-hidden secret, it still concerns all human beings. It is therefore unveiled for all to see. Not only that, but it is revealed in plain language as well, intelligible to everyone, educated or not. We recognize this in part through the verbs used in various letters to refer to the spreading of this information: instruct, enlighten, make aware, make known, speak of, reveal, give knowledge of, and so on. All of them point to effective communication.

We also see it in the way the letter writers identify the formal subject of this communication. In the earliest text about the secret, Paul says more than once that it stands at the core of his apostolic speech and proclamation (1 Cor 2:1–10). In Romans he says the same thing (Rom 16:25). The author of Colossians, for his part, professes to proclaim the gospel, whose servant he has become (Col 1:23). He shortly adds that he announces the recently revealed secret (vv. 26–28), and later again, that he "declare[s] the mystery of Christ" (4:3). This secret is thus synonymous with the gospel he preaches. In his turn, the author of Ephesians identifies the content of the secret (Eph 3:3–4, 9) with the gospel itself (vv. 6–7). Thus later on he can speak of "the mystery of the gospel" (6:19), that is, the secret revealed by the gospel.

To sum up, the two concepts of secret and gospel stand very near to one another. In fact, we can say they include each other; they are identical with each other in terms of their content. What is true of the one, that it is open, clear, and intelligible, is true also of the other. The gospel that from pedagogical motives was at first whispered in the ears of intimate disciples, would later be shouted from the rooftops, to be heard throughout the entire town (Matt 10:27).

Now, after this lengthy analysis, we are in a better position to grasp the primary characteristic of the Christian sense of mystery. It is not what the average person may imagine it to be. As we saw at the beginning of the chapter, people confuse this mystery with strange and cryptic things, with all sorts of odd phenomena. Many people act as if tangible reality actually concealed another reality behind it, the true reality, the only one worth paying attention to. In their eyes, it is as if below the surface of things there lay a subterranean net of meaning. They reduce our concrete world to a curtain on a stage and spend all their energy trying to sneak a look behind it.

Among these people is a host of writers and authors, above all perhaps those who belong to the romantic tradition, a tradition that at times has stood very close to occultism. Sensing the deeper dimensions of existence, these artists sought to reach its very limits. They loved vague boundaries. But true reality, in all its richness, is not to be found out there on the periphery. It is where it is: in the center, everywhere in fact. It is sufficient unto itself. A stone is a stone; a tree is a tree; a human being is a human being and nothing else. Of course, the sfumato of certain painters is imaginatively stimulating, and doubtless the hazy landscapes and blurred portraits by the impressionists have their charm. But true reality is not hidden in a metaphysical fog.

As Paul sees it, the world's true being does not lie hidden away in something like a secret desk drawer or in the false bottom of a suitcase. The mysterious nature of what he calls the mystery does not lie in its presumed unintelligibility. It is not something subtle, cabalistic, or cryptic, in need of deciphering. The secret is only inaccessible so long as it is not brought out into the light. As long as he wished it to be so, God's plan remained God's secret, a well-guarded secret that no one could have envisioned. No one could have foreseen it, for it depended on a divine decree, a free choice on God's part. God alone knew what his plan was for our deliverance, how in Christ he would welcome all humanity unto himself. He and only he was able to make that secret known, and only when he considered it appropriate to do so. But as soon as this unanticipated, unpredictable secret had been unveiled, it became accessible to everyone.

We know this from (among other things) what is said about those whom the gospel addresses and about how they received the message. In the Letter to the Colossians, for example, we are told that the Colossian readers have "the word of the truth, the gospel that has come to [them]" (Col 1:5–6a). They have "truly comprehended the grace of God" (v. 6b), which they have "learned from Epaphras" (v. 7), and they now know "how great among the Gentiles are the riches of the glory of this mystery" (v. 27). More specifically, they have "received Christ Jesus the Lord, [and now must] continue to live [their] lives in him, rooted and built up in him and established in the faith, just as [they] were taught" (Col 2:6–7). They have thus been duly instructed in what they need to know.

For a portion of humanity today, God remains silent. For Paul and his colleagues, he has spoken. He has left them a clear statement of his mind.

Chapter 8

A Mystery Concealed Forever

Like many people do, feeling the need for a mental break, you open a detective novel and begin to read. Maybe it is your weariness that makes you a little slow-witted and unobservant, but for some reason you find yourself led down one false trail after another. Time after time, you have to say to yourself, "No, the person I suspected can't be the murderer after all." If the author has done a good job, the unresolved tension increases the further you read, until at last you reach the solution, which brings with it a genuine sense of satisfaction. But the moment of contentment is short-lived. As soon as the puzzle is solved, your interest in it evaporates. The novel suddenly loses its value for you. Who would ever want to read it a second time?

This imaginary scene raises a general question: Must every unveiling of a secret lead to a corresponding letdown? Can we possibly imagine an unveiling that calls forth continuous joy instead, as well as continued searching? It seems to have been exactly this way within the Pauline School. The idea that a long-concealed secret has been revealed implies no sense of disappointment. Quite the contrary. It drives Paul, who has just revealed the secret of Israel's final destiny (Rom 11:25), to utter a burst of praise: "For from him and through him and to him are all things. To him be the glory forever. Amen" (v. 36). It leads him again, at the end of the letter, to exclaim: "[Glory] to the only wise God, through Jesus Christ, to whom be the glory forever! Amen" (Rom 16:27). The writer to the Ephesians likewise uses a doxology to round out his discourse on the revealed secret: "Now to him who by the power at work within us is able to accomplish abundantly far more than all we can ask or imagine, to him be glory in the church and in Christ Jesus to all generations, forever and ever. Amen" (Eph 3:20–21).

Here, then, we have an unveiling that leads to long-lasting joy. How does it happen that we find ourselves standing between two such contradictory results: on the one hand, disappointment, and on the other, excitement? Could it perhaps be explained by the fact that the one case, a crime to be solved, represents a human situation, while the other is a divine mystery? Put more precisely, can it rest on the fact that a human mystery is finite and the divine mystery is infinite?

IN THE PRESENCE OF MEASURELESS REALITIES

In the Pauline corpus, every time we hear about the divine mystery, we are said in fact to be standing in the presence of measureless realities. Two words frequently occur in this context, words otherwise semantically related to each other: "deep" and "riches." Let us take a closer look at this subject.

The first time Paul uses the Greek term *mystērion,* referring to his proclamation of "God's wisdom, secret and hidden" (1 Cor 2:7), he says in the same breath that he proclaims "what no eye has seen, nor ear heard, nor the human heart conceived" (v. 9). From the very beginning, therefore, he has in mind something that defies our powers of conception. In the next verse he mentions "the depths of God," which the Spirit alone is able to search out (v. 10). Later again, in the Letter to the Romans, he presents the divine wisdom as fathomless: "O the depth of the riches . . . of God!" (Rom 11:33). Here once more Paul speaks of a depth that cannot be plumbed. There is no point in trying to measure that which knows no measure.

The other term, "riches," occurs especially often in the Prison Epistles. By disclosing this mystery, God has permitted the believers to know "how great among the Gentiles are the riches of the glory of this mystery" (Col 1:27). That is, they are given a glimpse of the overflowing abundance of God's glory that has been made available to the gentile world. This is echoed in the Letter to the Ephesians, where the author claims to have received grace to "bring to the Gentiles the news of the boundless riches of Christ" (Eph 3:8). In fact, the noun "riches" and the adjective "rich" occur more often in this letter than in any other. We hear of the rich grace through which God has "lavished on us" his wisdom and insight (Eph 1:6–8). His inheritance is "rich" (v. 18); his power is of "immeasurable greatness" (v. 19). He is moreover "rich in mercy" (2:4), his grace rich beyond measure (v. 7), his glory full of riches (3:16). Together, all these texts open up before us a perspective of dizzying proportions.

FROM IGNORANCE TO IGNORANCE

So there is a great difference between the mystery resolved at the end of a detective novel and the mystery presented in these letters. This is true in spite of a certain common denominator, namely that each in its way leads us from ignorance to understanding. What a detective story reveals is merely the identity of the murderer. A simple name, his or hers, is all it takes to satisfy us. The answer is thus clear-cut, though a bit meager perhaps; or, if you like, it is flat and two-dimensional. Once it is out, the entire reality is unveiled.

At first glance, the unveiling of a divine mystery seems to be equally clear-cut. This mystery is unveiled indeed; it is revealed, or made known, as various texts put it. The revelation is formulated in ordinary, plain, and commonly used terms. It can be summed up with brevity, as in Ephesians 3:3. We are thus properly informed about it. But this does not mean that the subject is exhaustively treated the moment the information is imparted to us. On the contrary, its content is full of ambiguities and puzzles, simply because of its depth and richness.

Louis-Marie Dewailly, according to his commentator Chantal Reynier, makes an interesting observation. The fact that something still remains hidden in this revealed mystery is in part reflected in the two different temporal indicators Paul uses at the end of Romans. When he says that a mystery "is now disclosed" and "made known" (Rom 16:26), both verbs are in the aorist, a tense that points to something that happened at a particular point in time, once for all. But when he says that the mystery "was kept secret for long ages" (v. 25), he uses the perfect tense, which refers to a state of affairs remaining in effect. He is not dealing, then, with something belonging exclusively to the past. In one sense, the mystery remains hidden. God has not abandoned his silence. He has revealed himself, true enough, but he has not revealed himself completely.

Lars Hartman, moreover, notes another text, this one from Colossians, in which we read that what has been said remains unsaid: "For I want you to know how much I am struggling for you, and . . . for all who have not seen me face to face. I want their hearts to be encouraged . . . so that they may have all the riches of assured understanding and have the knowledge of God's mystery, that is, Christ himself, in whom are hidden all the treasures of wisdom and knowledge" (Col 2:1–3). Hidden! In other words, these treasures are, in Christ, hoarded away and inaccessible. Consequently, we must reckon with riches that remain hidden. On the one hand, the mystery is revealed. On the other hand, it remains hidden away, and the knowledge of it remains forever something to strive after. God has in fact made known his glorious riches in the mystery of Christ (1:27). Yet all the treasures of wisdom and understanding remain hidden in this same Christ.

But what exactly is it that has remained hidden for so long and now at last is spoken? It is what we have already seen: that God's salvation is offered to all humanity, without distinction; that his merciful compassion is universal. This is easily put into plain speech and easy to understand. What, then, is it that remains unspoken? What is it that will never be fully understood? It is what hides behind God's merciful decree (Rom 11:32), the reason for it, its origin, its fundamental assumption, namely the wisdom of God (v. 33a). It is this that remains forever "mysterious" (1 Cor 2:7). It is this that characterizes him who is "the only wise God" (Rom 16:27). It is precisely this mystery's inscrutability that makes Paul's rhetorical questions about it forever unanswerable (Rom 11:33–35). We have finally arrived then at an irreducible remainder.

What name can we legitimately give to this mysterious remainder, which must for all time to come remain unknowable? The Greek term *mystērion* can be translated in two ways, depending on context. Where the issue has to do with something kept hidden, we can use the word "secret." But once the hidden thing has been revealed, the term "secret" is no longer appropriate. An unveiled secret is a secret no longer. We need to find another term, one that corresponds to what remains inaccessible even after its unveiling. For this we should use the word "mystery."

A mystery is always a mystery, impenetrable no matter how much we try to plumb its depths or how much we say or write about it. Its rich content offers a perpetual challenge to all such attempts. However much God may reveal of his secret, of his plan for deliverance, he remains silent about what lies behind this plan. Of course, he does lead us from ignorance to understanding, but at the same time he leads us also from ignorance to deeper ignorance. It cannot be otherwise, unless we want to make a liar of King Solomon, when, on the day he saw the temple filled with smoke, he said, "The LORD has said that he would dwell in thick darkness" (1 Kgs 8:12).

THE PARTICULAR NATURE OF THE CHRISTIAN SENSE OF MYSTERY

We are now able, better than before, to appreciate the difference between a crime to be solved, or any problem of the sort, and, on the other hand, a mystery. A puzzle is something we solve once for all. A mystery is something we sound the depths of, something to immerse ourselves in, over and over again. Against the background of the texts we have been discussing, we now have a better means for discerning the particular nature of Christian believers. They distinguish themselves alike from both skeptics and fanatics, and from those opposing attitudes to reality. The cool, indifferent skeptics cannot deal with any form of definitive knowledge. They are firmly locked up in their "maybe or maybe not" approach. Thus they know nothing at all. Fanatics, however, claim to know everything and to know it better than anyone else does. In their intolerant fundamentalism, they do not perceive reality's complexity. They are and remain imprisoned in the snares of black-and-white thinking. People like this frighten away a host of honest truth-seekers, who stand at a distance for fear of finding themselves pigeonholed.

In contrast to skeptics, believers know they have been led from ignorance to understanding. The divine secret has indeed been revealed for them. But they also realize they have been brought at the same time from ignorance to further ignorance. God's mystery remains forever impenetrable, even for them. Of course they realize that God is wise, but they acknowledge that they do not know what this means, or how wise he is, or to what degree. This is exactly what was meant by Thomas Aquinas, a theologian who in no way could be accused of defeatism in the pursuit of knowledge. Aquinas wrote, somewhat provocatively: "Neither the catholic nor the pagan understands God's being as it truly is."

Chapter 9

Penetrating the Cloud of Unknowing

If the riches found in Christ are "boundless" (Eph 3:8), it is worth asking whether there is any point at all in trying to plumb their depths. What is inscrutable is doubtless inscrutable for all time.

Yet we do not need to feel paralyzed by this. We may feel stimulated by it instead; it can waken our curiosity, in spite of the inscrutability. Even if we know that we shall never exhaust the richness of the divine mystery, we wonder whether it might still be possible to grasp at least something of it. And even a limited understanding of this "something" can be considered of more value than any full-orbed knowledge of a host of less important things. The members of the Pauline circle must have had some consciousness of this, since understanding occupies such an important place in such letters as Colossians and Ephesians. Not only that, but they also present this highly desirable knowledge, *gnōsis,* as something that develops, something that can grow. Its first, elementary stage entices us to push all the more deeply into the divine mystery. It is precisely progress in this knowledge that both letters recommend.

A GRADUAL PENETRATION OF THE MYSTERY

What does the author of Colossians say about this? To begin, he reminds his readers of their past: "You have heard of this hope before in the word of the truth, the gospel . . . from the day you heard it and truly comprehended the grace of God" (Col 1:5–6). But this foundational knowledge, resulting from the first missionary proclamation, is not enough. More is needed: "We have not ceased praying for you and asking that you may be filled with the knowledge of God's will in all spiritual wisdom and understanding, so that you may lead lives worthy of the Lord, fully pleasing to him, as you bear fruit in every good work" (vv. 9–10). Here the author desires among his readers an increase in ethical discernment, in the knowledge of God's will. It is the same a bit further on, when he writes, "Do not lie to one another, seeing that you have stripped off the old self with its practices and have clothed yourselves with the new self, which is being renewed in knowledge according to the image of its creator" (Col 3:9–10).

In the same way, the writer of Ephesians urges his readers "to be renewed in the spirit of [their] minds, and to [clothe themselves] with the new self, created according to the likeness of God in true righteousness and holiness" (Eph 4:23–24). In certain texts, then, we hear of a process of moral maturation, of an ever better informed practical discernment that leads to an increasingly holy way of life.

In still other texts we hear of a purely intellectual maturity, or we might say a life of increased contemplation. The author of Colossians writes, "I became [the church's] servant according to God's commission that was given to me for you, to make the word of God fully known" (Col 1:25). And he adds, "For I want [all of you to] . . . have all the riches of assured understanding and [to] have the knowledge of God's mystery, that is, Christ himself" (Col 2:1–2). We meet the same wish for a gradual, contemplative penetration of God's being in the parallel letter: "I pray that the God of our Lord Jesus Christ, the Father of glory, may give you a spirit of wisdom and revelation as you come to know him" (Eph 1:17). Further along we read again of the desire for a clearer understanding of God's mystery (3:16–19).

Over and over, then, it is expected that the readers will be filled "with all spiritual wisdom and insight," that they will be "renewed in true knowledge," that they will be "renewed in spiritual understanding," and so on. If these readers had been tempted at times to think they were full-grown and fully taught, such repeated prayers and desires should certainly have contributed to renewing their openness to further development. They are thus faced with a kind of continual disruption of their assumptions. How does this gradual penetration of the mystery take place, understood in concrete terms? We may begin to answer this question by thinking through the various roles that words generally play for the writer and his readers.

LAST AND FIRST

Literary artists strive to express what they perceive, what they feel and think. With determined persistence, they pursue adequate and living ways of putting into words what they bear within them. After something like an exhausting pregnancy, they give birth at last to a publishable product born of an extended creative process. With writers, then, the words come last.

For Christians it is the reverse: the words come first. We come to faith through hearing (Rom 10:14–17), or through reading. In one sense Christianity is a religion of scripture, in the same way as Judaism and Islam are each founded upon a book. The faithful take as their point of departure an authoritative text, which they regard as inspired. They consider themselves completely dependent on a revelation viewed as originating from the outside. From the beginning, then, Bible readers have understood what they have been instructed to believe in and to live by. This fact alone should be enough to initiate them into the deeper mystery, but things are not quite so simple.

In spite of all their diligent efforts, secular writers must eventually acknowledge that they never really find the right words in which to clothe their experiences. When they consider the gaping distance between the books they dreamed of writing and the actual results of their labors, they can hardly regard their literary works as anything but a series of failures. Even though they make repeated improvements in order to reduce the distance between what they envisioned and what they have actually produced, the finished product never measures up to the dream. Awareness of this is a constant source of agony for a writer. If anyone can be said to know how difficult it is to write, writers can!

However, those who have been wakened to faith know how difficult it is to read, to really read a text—that is, to bring forth from it what is actually there. But even believers are aware of a certain distance, in this case the distance between the written words before their eyes and what those words are meant to convey. The distance between sign and signified is in fact a large one, both for the author and for the readers. This is true, even though the movement from the one to the other goes in opposite directions: authors move from a previous experience to a written account drawn up afterward; readers, in contrast, move from an existing text to a subsequent experience. If it takes time for a writer to master his own language or to find his own style, it takes an equally long time and just as much patience for a pious reader to really apply herself to a biblical text. (The fact that this seemingly straightforward, easy task of reading is actually difficult and tedious finds living proof in all the contemplative monks and nuns. If it were not so difficult, why would they occupy their entire lives with it?)

Reading a text rightly is thus no easy process, because, for one thing, words are merely words, empty shells, air. They are nothing but conventional, abstract signs, even those used for referring to concrete realities. Words are disembodied, transparent, and hollow. We cannot take a seat on the word "chair," or warm ourselves at the word "bonfire," or find shelter from the rain under the word "roof." No one can commit a murder by using the word "murder," except perhaps in the writing of a detective novel. And what does the word "smell" smell like? Or how do the words "sweet" and "bitter" taste? Between all these words and their corresponding realities yawns an abyss we cannot easily cross over. Only reality itself is real. Reality alone is worthy of our attention, even if it is difficult to attain it from the words representing it. So what are we to do?

PRELIMINARY PRECISION

A first step in addressing this situation can consist in defining the words used, by Paul for example, so that we can understand what he is talking about. The primary thing about a definition is that it teaches us the exact meaning of a word. But definitions also have a disadvantage. By offering us a sharply contoured framework, a definition can lull us into confidence that we have exhausted a word's richness. But this is misleading, especially when we are dealing with divine realities. As we can see from the Latin root of the word "definition"—*finis*/limit—a "de-fini-tion" puts delimitations on something, delimiting it from something else. And if it delimits, it also confines. But the mystery of God is limitless. It cannot be fenced in by any kind of boundary marker. As Gregory of Nyssa put it, "The only limit God knows is the absence of any limit." Thus a definition can be misleading.

Under no circumstances can a definition be completely satisfying, since it never tells the entire story. Precision is good. Precision is useful, even necessary, if we do not want to wander around in a fog. But precision is not everything. A word or a concept does not merely have a particular contour. It also has something we could call density, quality, and depth. Within the narrow borders of a definition it is thus always possible to go deeper. If we do not do so, we are only half the way there. The text remains partly mute. So how can we get the text to speak?

INDIVIDUAL RESPONSIBILITY

Getting the half-mute words to say something to us requires another step beyond framing a definition. What is that next step? The information we find in the New Testament is public, collective, addressed to all humanity. But any text, biblical or secular, attains its full value only when an individual reader receives it. It is incumbent upon every believer to take responsibility for his or her own relationship with the text. Of course, the objective message can certainly be heard in community with other believers, during the liturgy, for example. But it cannot be appropriated except in solitude, in isolation. No one can do it for another person. The message can be taken in only through a personal consciousness, through what was once called *lectio divina*. Only then is our wonder kept alive, and only then is the text still able to speak to our hearts. But how does this individual reception actually happen?

Without blaming anyone in particular, we can declare quite categorically that nowadays we in the so-called West live in an age of speed. Our cars, trains, boats, and planes travel at ever faster rates. Thanks to e-mail and other technical means, our messages reach the other side of the planet virtually instantaneously. We ourselves are always in a hurry. We close our letters "in all haste"!

This accelerated tempo can also be seen at the intellectual level. Courses are available in speed-reading, teaching people how to scan a text. This method is especially useful for skimming an administrative or economic report. The question is, however, whether it is equally useful when applied to texts of another kind, let us say poetical or meditative texts in which rhythm, pitch, or atmosphere says as much as the individual words do. If we want to read such texts profitably, we should perhaps try to read them as ancient readers did. They read with both eye and ear, and with the lips. That is, they read aloud, or at least half-aloud, even when they read to themselves. This is exactly what the Ethiopian queen's finance minister was doing, riding along in his chariot somewhere between Jerusalem and Gaza. And because he was reading aloud, Philip the deacon, making his way along the same road, was able to recognize the text from the prophet Isaiah, which the man was reading (Acts 8:26–27).

Those of us who read silently and quickly, too quickly, would surely come out ahead by simply putting on the brakes. One way to do this perhaps is to read a text over again, many times one after another. Or we might read aloud, even softly, as in a mantra, until we begin to taste the text on the tongue. Read and reread. Chew. Ruminate. But will even that be enough? Let us once more consider the difference between a poet and her reader. The function of the poet's words is to reflect her personal experience. The words a believer finds in Holy Scripture, however, have a different role. Their function is to awaken in the believer a similar personal experience. They help the reader to experience something new. Yet, though it may be a new experience, it is based on something old. As we let the words sink into our consciousness and work there in silence, we can with good advantage recall to mind earlier privileged moments when certain biblical words and images opened themselves to us. In this way, these earlier experiences can be renewed and strengthened, and the distance between the words and the reality they represent can be reduced.

Their repeated urgings toward ever deeper and richer insight imply that Paul and his fellow workers recognized at least the possibility of reducing this distance between word and reality. We thus have permission to dream of a day when the inspired words we read will reveal to us all the more the substance of their meaning, and thereby inspire us! The written text itself is a given. What remains is to discover the spirit that dwells within them. After an objective analysis the time comes for a warmly vivid realization. Then the words can become more what they are meant to be—that is, something more closely identical with the reality they represent, such that this reality becomes clear, tangible, almost sculptural, as in a literary masterpiece. Truly skillful writers can do magic with words, changing the word "water" into water and making the word "sun" give forth light and warmth. Good writers can write in such a way that the tree they are describing actually casts a shadow. Taught by teachers such as these, we succeed in glimpsing the reality hiding behind the biblical words we read. These then become living words, and through them, we also live.

But once more we ask, how does this come to pass? Perhaps there is something we can learn from the experiments our forebears conducted in this regard.

DENIAL AND HYPERAFFIRMATION

According to long-standing tradition, two works, called *On the Divine Name* and *On the Mystical Theology,* were written by Dionysios the Areopagite, the Athenian philosopher whom Paul converted to Christianity (Acts 17:34). But the tradition lacks support. At the earliest, these works were composed during the sixth century. Nonetheless, they exercised a profound influence on later theology, both in the East and in the West. In the thirteenth century, Thomas Aquinas used them as a basis for his meditations on the possibility of speaking about God while simultaneously respecting his inespressible nature. In his own works Thomas reckoned with three approaches to the divine mystery—three "ways," as he called them: *via causalitatis, via negationis,* and *via eminentiae.* Simply put, he envisioned that in answer to the question "Is God such and such?" we would first answer, "yes." Then we would answer, "no," and finally, "yes, of course, but only with qualification."

Thus, even if we are merely fumbling for an acceptable understanding of God, we can begin with a positive affirmation. If we are convinced that everything derives from a Creator, we may take it for granted that the positive characteristics and abilities found in creation have their corresponding features in him. Consider what the psalmist thought about it: "He who planted the ear, does he not hear? He who formed the eye, does he not see?" (Ps 94:9). The question of whether God has the ability to see, hear, or know can thus be answered with an unhesitating "yes." Going backward in this way, from the creaturely effect to the divine cause (Latin: *causa*), and expecting to find there in the divine sphere the best of what we have here on earth, is exactly what is meant by the *via causalitatis.* So far, so good.

But suppose we read a biblical text describing God's exalted state, this one from Isaiah, for instance: "For as the heavens are higher than the earth, so are my ways higher than your ways and my thoughts than your thoughts" (Isa 55:9). If we take it seriously, we are gripped with doubt, with something like shame for having fallen victim to an illusion. We catch ourselves creating a god in our own image. We cry out in terror that God is something "other," and that we did not know it! As soon as we realize our mistake, we hasten to take back what we just said in a moment of thoughtlessness. We promptly declare, no, God cannot be viewed as being or doing anything whatever in a human way. Every attempt to describe him must be rejected. He is neither this, nor that, nor that. This sort of denial, which comes close to mere silence, characterizes the *via negationis,* or *via negativa,* as it is also called.

But this *via negativa,* which has lately become a kind of theological "fad," can hardly be the last word on the subject. At the end of the day, we may still wonder whether, in spite of everything, God does indeed possess the characteristics we attributed to him in the beginning. No human being who has sensed his immensity and become fascinated with it can long keep silent. The very attractiveness of God drives such a person to leave all denials behind and to risk resorting to other means of expressing it, such as hyperaffirmation. This involves our elevating words to their optimal level and beyond, if possible. We give them extra freight, as it were. We do this, for example, by adding such prefixes as *hyper* or *super.* Words with these prefixes point hyperbolically outside of themselves. They do not say all there is to say; it is impossible to do so in any case. Yet they function as incentives, signaling the direction in which we should turn our attention, upward, and beyond. In a desperate attempt to speak the unspeakable, we labor in this way to find language that surpasses even itself. We try to maximize it, to stretch it to the breaking point. Naturally, God is not this or that in the same way we might be. Still, perhaps he is so in the eminent degree. And for this reason the third approach is called *via eminentiae.* We therefore now make any necessary adjustments and nuance the radical conclusions we have arrived at so far in the foregoing stages.

The tripartite approach described above is actually indivisible. It is, moreover, so important that it will repay us to review it once more in order to be more precise about the nature of each of the three steps.

There is not a great deal to say about the first, apart from the fact that it corresponds to a spontaneous, innocent, even naive stage of the process. By itself it is certainly insufficient to the task, but it lays the groundwork, making the other two stages possible.

Moving on a step further, fully conscious that no one can come even near to understanding what God's character is really like, we determinedly dismiss out of hand all conceivable suggestions. We eliminate a priori all positive qualifiers we could ever think of. None of them would suffice, not even the most sublime. In the face of such a chain of impossibilities, we can make only lists of what we reject. Believers who radically throw off every statement about God are living on the safe side. They run no risk of saying something stupid, something blasphemous, about him. Leaving things unsaid is doubtless the safest way of doing justice to what cannot be spoken. This *via negativa,* the way of unknowing, can be regarded as the stage of trial, or judgment.

Finally, we come to the last step, one that is risky enough, to be sure, but one that is justified nonetheless. Provided we guard ourselves against unduly simplified formulations, which would reveal fatal misconceptions, we can make bold to draw comparisons with the incomparable. This third stage can be seen as a stage of synthesis, uniting two seemingly irreconcilable attitudes: yes and no.

Still, it clearly and markedly deviates from the second stage. The second is static, whereas the third is dynamic. The *via negativa* is in fact no "way" at all in the sense of a way we can follow step-by-step, a way that leads us gradually toward our goal. For every solution is ruled out from the start. There is no hierarchy there, no gradation. The highest and foremost "names"—to use the language of Dionysius—are as useless as the least of them. Nothing, absolutely nothing, is acceptable. Halfway along we realize we are just as far from the goal as we were when we set out. We are only marching in place, merely treading water.

The *via eminentiae,* on the other hand, is a true "way." We move along an ascending scale, where qualifications such as wisdom, generosity, and strength—applied to God—take on an ever increasing dignity. We progress from affirmation to affirmation, seamlessly, unendingly. The higher we go in this, the more we approach the divine reality, our anticipation and curiosity mounting all the while. In spite of these crescendos, we remain conscious of the fact that the similarity between the Creator and the creation is only relative, while the difference between them is radical. The way *(modus)* in which God is wise, generous, and so on, remains completely impenetrable. And thanks to this reservation—a streak of denial in the heart of our affirmation—his transcendence is honored.

Finally, we may note that the *via negativa* is ascetic in the extreme. It would be prohibitively puritanical, fatally pure, if it stood alone. How long can we live in a vacuum, after all? It needs to be complemented by the *via eminentiae,* which is cautiously generous and indulgent, provided we do not lose sight of God's majesty in the process. This third "way" leaves greater space for wonder, for a far more joyful wonder. It presents God as eminently desirable.

Obviously Paul had no opportunity to read either Dionysius the Areopagite or Thomas Aquinas. Moreover, their scholastic way of reasoning (shall we say) would have been foreign to him. Yet numerous expressions and turns of phrase can be found in his letters that reveal how spontaneously and purely intuitively he followed the same scheme as they did. That scheme surely reflects both the structure of our psyche and the nature of reality.

What would later come to be called the *via causalitatis* was not unknown to Paul. One indicator of this is what he wrote to the Romans: "Ever since the creation of the world [God's] eternal power and divine nature, invisible though they are, have been understood and seen through the things he has made" (Rom 1:20). Paul had already taken the phenomena of the visible world as a place from which to mount up to the knowledge of the Most High.

But it is equally clear that he takes into consideration the limits of our intellectual abilities. This is why he often uses so-called privative adjectives, which in English translation begin with prefixes *un-* or *in-* or end with the suffix *-less*. We have just seen the term "invisible," for example; others he uses include "imperishable," "incomprehensible," and "boundless." At the same time he uses expressions that disregard those limitations. His epistles swarm with hyperbolic words, beginning with the Greek prefix *hyper-,* which come into English as "abound all the more" (Rom 5:20; "superabound") and "[glory] beyond all measure" (2 Cor 4:17), to mention only two. Add to these his many references to thoughts of riches and overflowing.

Now, with a perspective renewed through the interpretive keys found in Dionysius and Thomas, it will presumably be easier to get some of the important words in the Pauline corpus to open themselves for us.

Chapter 10

The Practice of Looking Backward

We read a text, or so we think, and we think we understand it. What we are seldom aware of, however, is that a text says more than we realize. By this I do not mean to say that a text necessarily includes hidden cryptic messages. Biblical texts are not usually made up of difficult words, of hermetic terms common in theological jargon. Ordinarily they are composed of typical words we can find in any dictionary. Yet those words can say more than what they seem to say at the first reading.

Any literary person will affirm that it is not easy to read a text, really read it straight from the page, and get it to divulge its full significance. Experts in this field distinguish between a basic reading skill and well-differentiated one.

It is a relatively simple thing to learn to read. Children can do it. In this electronic age, even machines can do it. Significantly more difficult is acquiring the ability to discern a text's deeper meaning, so that the printed words transform themselves into a living reality and the author's rapture becomes the reader's as well. It requires diligent practice. This kind of skill in reading is particularly called for in cases of texts that deal with God's mystery. Everything we have learned about this mystery up to now amounts to virtually nothing, compared to what remains to be learned.

It sometimes happens that concrete circumstances lead Paul to look backward. When he wants to characterize for the Corinthians the role he and his coworkers fulfill in their congregation, he asks that they consider himself and the others as "stewards of God's mysteries" (1 Cor 4:1). When he describes his own personal role, he says that he came to them in order to announce the "mystery of God" (2:1). The best thing he has to offer them, then, is the mystery of God, which, as we have seen, is synonymous with God's universal plan of salvation (Rom 16:25–27; cf. Col 1:25–27; Eph 1:9–13 and 3:1–11).

This plan was not self-evident. No one had anticipated it; it was completely unexpected by humanity, and long kept secret by God. When it was finally disclosed, it was viewed as shocking, not least of all by Jews. People wondered what could possibly lie behind it. What could have motivated God to intervene in such an astounding way?

To answer this very question, Paul sometimes looks backward and lays his finger on the plan's presupposition, or rather on its prehistory, even though that lies beyond the boundaries of time, deep in the eternal bosom of God. He then makes use of various words that all point to virtually the same thing. He speaks of God's "grace" (especially in Romans 4 and 5), of his "kindness" (Rom 11:22), even of "his kindness and forbearance and patience" (Rom 2:4), or of his generous "gifts" (Rom

11:29; 1 Cor 2:12). Most often he speaks of his "mercy"—
a word that subsumes all these divine characteristics. The
doctrinal portion of Romans deals precisely with this all-
encompassing attribute (Rom 3:21–11:36). When the apostle
summarizes this idea one last time in Romans 11:32–33 ("For
God has imprisoned all [human beings] in disobedience so
that he may be merciful to all"), he bursts out in the well-
known words, "O the depth of the riches and wisdom and
knowledge of God!" What actually strikes him with astonishment, then, is the wisdom and knowledge of God. In his search
for the source of God's bewildering decision to save all humanity, Paul first looks back to God's mercy. But he does not
stop there; he goes even further back, until he reaches the ultimate source, divine wisdom.

The significance that the mysterious side of God's nature
has for Paul is obvious from the detailed way he discusses it the
first time it comes up in his letters (1 Cor 1:15–2:16). Likewise
significant is the fact that it is mentioned in the three main
Pauline texts treating the revealed mystery (1 Cor 2:6–10; Rom
16:25–27; and Eph 3:8–12). Thus we are dealing here with a
core term in the proclamation of the Pauline School, a word to
take note of, a word to remember, a word on which to spend
some time. Unfortunately it is an abstract word, and anything
abstract is easily seen as pale and unreal. How can we give it
living substance? What would "God's wisdom" mean for us if
it meant what it is intended to mean?

WISDOM IN THE OLD TESTAMENT

We can easily show that Paul seldom cites the Old Testament as often and as densely as he does when he is discussing
this divine characteristic. For this reason it seems natural first
of all to take a brief look at how God's wisdom was viewed in
ancient Israel. It was usual to use human wisdom as a point of

departure. But how was that viewed? Beginning with concrete and unpretentious, perhaps even lowly, everyday experience, we find texts where wisdom is equated with the professional skill of a craftsman (Exod 31:1–5; Isa 28:24–29), or where is it connected with the accomplishments of current technology (Job 28:1–14)—something worthy of high praise.

Moving to the top of the social ladder, we find sometimes a skilled governor, such as Joseph in Egypt (Gen 41 and 47), sometimes an honored king in Israel, one who can attend to the law and justice (1 Kgs 10:9; Sir 10:1). Solomon was regarded as preeminent in this respect. The young man who had recently taken his place on the throne considered himself green and inexperienced (1 Kgs 3:7). For this reason he prayed for "an understanding mind" (v. 9). Then God said to him, "Because you have asked this, and have not asked for yourself long life or riches, or for the life of your enemies, but have asked for yourself understanding to discern what is right, I now do according to your word. Indeed I give you a wise and discerning mind; no one like you has been before you and no one like you shall arise after you" (1 Kgs 3:11–12). Here once more we are dealing primarily with a practical wisdom—again something worthy of appreciation.

At a more general level, this time from a moral perspective, we can view wisdom as the art of living, as the ability to direct one's own life by readily paying attention to the experiences of one's elders. A wise man is able to esteem things in line with their actual worth and then to act accordingly. Both the Book of Proverbs and the Psalter preserve several ideal portraits of such people. All these texts are permeated with a clear admiration. Whether in connection with a craftsman, a king, or an individual person of faith, human wisdom is portrayed as something worth having, something actually given by God (Gen 41:38–39)—something worth praying for.

But there are some people who overvalue their own perceived wisdom. Various spiritual leaders warn against such in-
flated self-opinions. Isaiah writes, "[Woe to] you who are wise
in your own eyes, and shrewd in your own sight!" (Isa 5:21).
And in Proverbs we read, "Do you see persons wise in their
own eyes? There is more hope for fools than for them" (Prov
26:12). There are many such texts in the Old Testament. Especially relevant in our context is the passage in Isaiah where the
prophet has the Lord promising to strike people with astonishment. What then results from this unexpected intervention?
"The wisdom of their wise shall perish, and the discernment of
the discerning shall be hidden" (Isa 29:14). This very verse is
the one Paul first quotes (rather freely, as he often does), when
he takes on the arrogance of Corinthians and contrasts human
wisdom with divine wisdom: "I will destroy the wisdom of the
wise, and the discernment of the discerning I will thwart"
(1 Cor 1:19).

THE FOOLISHNESS OF GOD
1 CORINTHIANS 1:18–2:16

With good reason, the apostle referred to such texts no
fewer than six times as he lectured the Corinthians. These
Christians had been behaving like children, pretending to be
"intellectual" and wrangling with each other over who had the
best teacher, so that they could boast. Paul felt it necessary to
put them in their place, and he does so energetically with a particularly eloquent polemic.

> Consider your own call, brothers and sisters: not many of you
> were wise by human standards, not many were powerful, not
> many were of noble birth. But God chose what is foolish in the
> world to shame the wise; God chose what is weak in the world
> to shame the strong; God chose what is low and despised in

the world, things that are not, to reduce to nothing things that are, so that no one might boast in the presence of God . . . as it is written, "Let the one who boasts, boast in the Lord." (1 Cor 1:26–31)

It must have been a salutary lesson for the Corinthians to see themselves equated with things that are not, with despised and weak things, with what the world considered foolish. Still, further on as he rounds out his argument with a practical conclusion, Paul shows no hesitation in once again seeking support from the older wisdom literature: "Do not deceive yourselves. If you think that you are wise in this age, you should become fools so that you may become wise. For the wisdom of this world is foolishness with God. For it is written, 'He catches the wise in their craftiness,' and again, 'The Lord knows the thoughts of the wise, that they are futile'" (1 Cor 3:18–20). With these two new quotations, one from Job 5:13 and the other from Psalm 94:11, Paul warns his addressees to reassess their view of wisdom.

Paul is just as provocative when he writes about the content of the message:

For the message about the cross is foolishness to those who are perishing, but to us who are being saved it is the power of God. . . . Has not God made foolish the wisdom of the world? For since, in the wisdom of God, the world did not know God through wisdom, God decided, through the foolishness of our proclamation, to save those who believe. For Jews demand signs and Greeks desire wisdom, but we proclaim Christ crucified, a stumbling block to Jews and foolishness to Gentiles, but to those who are the called, both Jews and Greeks, Christ the power of God and the wisdom of God. For God's foolishness is wiser than human wisdom, and God's weakness is stronger than human strength. (1 Cor 1:18–25)

Paul's audacity seems to know no bounds. It is not enough that in discussing the question of humankind, he paradoxically insists that it is the despised and disdained who are chosen. But he does the same thing when he speaks of God: he declares God's weakness, obvious in the seemingly final defeat of Christ, as power, and God's foolishness as wisdom.

His use of these outrageous paradoxes must be explained on the basis of how he views human failure. Human beings had in their hands the possibility of learning to know God through ordinary human wisdom, that is, through looking at the created world. For the world was surrounded and permeated by the wisdom of God and bore witness to it (1 Cor 1:21; cf. Rom 1:19–22). But they missed the opportunity. When this more obvious, ordinary way led humanity nowhere, God chose an unordinary way—one of madness in human eyes. He chose to redeem the world through a disgraceful execution on a cross—which Paul gladly mentions whenever he looks back (here in 1 Cor 1:23; 2:2, and in Gal 1:3; 3:1). As he sees it, God's wisdom—that is, his ingenuity, his daring inventiveness—is so great that it overwhelms its antithesis. In the same way, an extremely bright light blinds the eye and is transformed into darkness. Too much is too much! But when wisdom is at its greatest, it cannot be described otherwise than by means of its opposite: a non-wisdom, an anti-wisdom, a foolishness.

If we want an even clearer idea of what Paul means by divine wisdom, we need to take another look at his summary statement: "For God's foolishness is wiser than human wisdom, and God's weakness is stronger than human strength"

(1 Cor 1:25). He is apparently making a comparison, since he uses the comparative forms "wiser" and "stronger." It could be tempting therefore, in a thoughtless moment, to imagine that divine wisdom is a kind of improvement on human wisdom. But that would mean that we had transformed God into an idol. Such an illusion is foreign to Paul, for he does not say here that God is wiser than human beings. Rather, he writes that the wisdom of God is foolishness. With this defiant formulation, he excludes any conceivable comparison that would bring the two realities anywhere near each other.

His way of recasting the concept is therefore synonymous with decisive repudiation: No! God is indeed wise, but not as humans are. Thus Paul in his own way takes what Dionysius the Areopagite would later call the *via negativa*.

"O THE DEPTH . . ."
ROMANS 11:33–36

In his first text on wisdom, motivated by the situation in Corinth, Paul had fun, as it were. He juggled with the concepts, replacing them with each other. But in his second text on the topic, the one found in Romans 11:33–36, Paul abandons the role of a juggler or an acrobat for that of a poet. Instead of provoking his readers with outrageous paradoxes, he speaks only very briefly. Yet the rich passage deserves to be read one more time.

> O the depth of the riches and wisdom and knowledge of God! How unsearchable are his judgments and how inscrutable his ways! "For who has known the mind of the Lord? Or who has been his counselor?" "Or who has given a gift to him, to receive a gift in return?" For from him and through him and to him are all things. To him be the glory forever. Amen. (Rom 11:33–36)

The style here is different from that of the earlier epistle, though Paul's basic outlook is the same. One sign of this similar outlook is the fact that among the texts he cites, this one appears in both letters: "For who has known the mind of the Lord? Or who has been his counselor?" (Rom 11:34; 1 Cor 2:16). In both cases Paul is standing in the presence of something that upsets all our calculations, though the actual reason for his confusion is different in each situation.

In 1 Corinthians, Paul is amazed at God's perplexing inventiveness in redeeming the world through the ignominious catastrophe of the cross. Here in Romans, however, he is amazed at another similarly perplexing detour, which he has just been discussing (chs. 9–11). He stands astonished at God's use of another failure, namely the Jewish refusal to recognize Jesus as Messiah, as a means to rescue the heathen. In both instances, he praises God's ingenuity. In both cases, the Portuguese proverb is proven true: God writes straight on crooked lines.

At this point, we may justifiably ask why Paul uses two words, "wisdom and knowledge," to describe the divine wisdom (Rom 11:33)? Is it because he wants to add emphasis by repetition, or strengthen his point with an apposition? Or is he actually referring to two separate realities?

Obviously the word "wisdom" carries a greater semantic weight than the word "knowledge" does. It is mentioned first, and appears again, alone, at the end of the letter (Rom 16:27). All things considered, we perhaps should not exaggerate the difference between them. It is minimal. Based on the word order in the two parallel parts of Romans 11:33, "wisdom" appears to refer more immediately to God's "decree," that is, to his universal plan of salvation. The plan expresses his inconceivable generosity toward all human beings, and forms the leading theme of the first main section of the epistle. As for the term "knowledge," it clearly refers more readily to God's "ways," that is, to his strategy, the means by which he accomplishes his purpose. In other words, he has used the temporary indifference of the Jews as a pretext for the conversion of the gentiles— the main theme of the two previous chapters. In both cases he is dealing with something no one has ever even dreamed of.

Here we are faced with further question: Why does Paul speak of "depth"? Why use this sort of metaphor? According to an Aristotelian axiom, there is nothing in the intellect that is not already found in the senses. This is doubtless true. Every time we think, we proceed from sensory perceptions. This is why we spontaneously use images, spatial images among others, even to describe emotional or spiritual realities. Some of these images are horizontal, as when we speak of close friends or distant relatives, or when we insist, "Far be it from me to do this or that!" Other images are vertical, as when we talk of a low motive or of lofty thoughts. And when we say that we are immersed in meditation, we are referring to a kind of deep-sea diving expedition into the fathomless complexity of reality, what the French call *l'épaisseur des choses*.

This leads us to think of an abyss, a gulf. In this respect it is synonymous with "deep," even "precipitously deep." It is exactly the word in the verse we have before us: "O the depth of the riches . . . !" The spiritual meaning of this outcry must certainly be Paul's amazement at how deep and rich God's wisdom is, or how deep it is because of his exceedingly great riches. God's ways are, in fact, "inscrutable." It will not help us to find an unusually long measuring line and play it out. All lines are too short, no matter how long they are! No matter how deep we let it go, it will never reach the bottom. Beneath every level lies another, and another, and still another, endlessly.

It is worth noting in this closing section of the didactic portion of Romans that Paul's admiration and wonder are actually called forth by impossibilities. The limits of our imaginative abilities are indicated by the rhetorical questions he asks: "Who has known the mind of the Lord? . . ." We have seen how he then finds inspiration from Old Testament texts, such as Jeremiah 23:18: "For who [of the prophets] has stood in the council of the LORD so as to see and to hear his word?" Paul could have appealed to several others, including the ironic question that Eliphaz puts to Job: "Have you listened in the council of God? And do you limit wisdom to yourself?" (Job 15:8).

Israel's wise often point out such shortcomings in the face of the mystery of wisdom. They do so probably because they see how easily we imagine that we understand it adequately. In order to dispel this illusion, we can follow with advantage the good advice of the Talmud: "If you want to understand the invisible, pay close attention to the visible." It is a fact that, even on the concrete level, we at times deceive ourselves into overestimating the power of our imagination. The Lord is portrayed as saying to Abraham, "Look toward heaven and count the stars, if you are able to count them" (Gen 15:5). But, of course, Abraham could not; neither can we. We cannot even grasp the significance of the distance between the stars, a distance measured in light-years. What does it really mean to us when we read that a light-year equals five quadrillion, eight hundred seventy-eight trillion miles, or that the sun weighs 1,989 billion billions of billion tons? Such astronomical sums defy our conceptual capabilities. We feel dizzy and fall silent in the knowledge that we grasp the nominal meaning of the words, but not the reality for which they stand.

The same thing is true when, with respect to divine wisdom, we read that it is literally incomprehensible. We cannot even think out the thought. No one can. Everyone we consult, from Paul to the older biblical authors, stand speechless. There is nothing else they can do. Even some modern writers are absolutely clear about the fitness of such a holy silence. We earlier saw Tomas Tranströmer speaking of "aphasia." His later collection *För levande och döda* (For the Living and the Dead) includes a poem called "Guldstekel," in which the poetic "I" warns against fanatical preachers who are all too sure about their subject: "How I detest the expression, one hundred percent of it!" In opposition to them he confesses, "We are in the church of silence, in the piety of wordlessness." In fact, the only sensible thing to do in the presence of divine wisdom is to keep quiet, or, like Paul, to confess and offer praise: "For from [God] and through him and to him are all things. To him be the glory forever. Amen" (Rom 11:36).

"... THE ONLY WISE GOD"
ROMANS 16:27

Thus a paean of praise climaxes this second of the three texts on divine wisdom found in letters doubtlessly written by Paul himself. The third and final of these texts does the same thing: "To the only wise God, through Jesus Christ, to whom be the glory forever! Amen" (Rom 16:27). Here, through yet another literary means, the apostle emphasizes this wisdom's inaccessibility. In the first text (1 Cor 1–2), he plays with paradoxes. In the second (Rom 11:33–36), he poses questions that remain unanswered. Both times the intention is to indicate the gulf yawning between God's wisdom and our inadequate perceptions of it. Now, as he looks backward for the last time, he speaks quite plainly—and quite laconically—of "the only wise God." His very taciturnity indicates how radically he dismisses every attempt at comparison.

In his own day, the author of the Book of Job wrote something quite in line with this: "Where then does wisdom come from? And where is the place of understanding? It is hidden from the eyes of all living, and concealed from the birds of the air. Abaddon and Death say, 'We have heard a rumor of it with our ears.' God understands the way to it, and he knows its place" (Job 28:20–23). Similarly, Isaiah writes, "'To whom then will you compare me, or who is my equal? says the Holy One" (Isa 40:25). And that is precisely the point: no comparison is possible. God is unique, incomparable, literally one of a kind when it comes to the way *(modus)* in which he is wise. Thoughts such as these are right in line with Paul's. In his first text he brazenly exchanges "wisdom" for "foolishness." In the second he speaks of a measureless deep and uses such privative adjectives as "unfathomable" and "inscrutable." The reality of this strikes him dumb with transported amazement. And then, not least of all, in the third text he excludes every conceivable comparison.

In all three cases, God's wisdom has no equal in the world with which we are familiar. In every case, God appears in one sense as an absent God. Thus, in these various ways, Paul shows what God is not. But can he truly do so without simultaneously revealing something about what God is?

Chapter 11

The Practice of Looking Forward

We live in the present. We have no other choice. Only the present is real. But what would the present be were it not for time gone by and time yet to come? How can we have the strength to live in the now without remembering what has gone before and without anticipating something of what is yet to be? We need to do this, not so that we may escape the present, but so that we may find support through the reassurance of memory and the energizing effect of anticipation. And in any case, do not the past and the future somehow belong together? Every beginning cries out for continuation, indeed for fulfillment.

This must be Paul's reasoning when he reminds the Corinthians of the "gifts bestowed on [them] by God" (1 Cor 2:12), that is, of the gifts they already possess. But he actually dwells more on coming gifts. Twice he mentions something looming on the horizon. That which "God has prepared for those who love him" (v. 9b), that which "God decreed before the ages for our glory" (v. 7), is something no human being would ever expect. We are thus promised a bright future, one that leads Paul, and us with him, to turn toward it, looking ahead.

He does this again in Romans when he speaks of those whom "[God] has prepared beforehand for glory" through his mercy, "including us whom he has called, not from the Jews only but also from the Gentiles" (Rom 9:32–24). According to Paul, then, it is our calling, our purpose, to have a part in the divine glory. What else does he have to say in Romans about this reality?

TWICE LOST

He actually begins with a tragedy. In his introduction, Paul describes the deplorable condition of humanity before God intervened. He summarizes by saying, "All have sinned and fall short of the glory of God" (Rom 3:23). But once he has presented God's forgiveness, his reconciliation, his justification (these three terms are synonymous), he is able to demonstrate that "we boast in our hope of sharing the glory of God" (Rom 5:2). Further along, with equal confidence, he once more mentions this same hope of glory (8:21–22) and assures that it will be revealed to us and made our own (v. 18). Thus, the reality of divine glory is first lost and then found again, at least in part. But it is also lost a second time, and in another sense: it is lost linguistically.

In the teaching section of Romans (chs. 1–11), the Greek word *doxa* ("glory") occurs a dozen times. The frequency itself reveals the value Paul places on glory. His distressed tone when he describes the disaster of losing it, as well as his triumphant tone when he presents the possibility of our regaining it completely, attest to the fact that for him glory involves something particularly valuable, something that stirs up luminous associations within us. What associations are these?

Let us give some thought to the way languages develop. Like many other things languages erode with time. Everything wears out, although some things wear out more quickly than others do; it is unavoidable. Coins that have been in circulation too long lose their originally sharp definition; so do words. One word that has especially suffered in this regard is none other than the word "glory." It has lost much of its former luster. It has paled; in fact, it has nearly "gone out."

In everyday speech the adjective "glorious" functions satisfactorily, as when we talk of glorious weather. But in the religious context it has acquired a strange tone, thanks to its misuse by certain excitable groups. Their bombastic jargon rings as false as does their programmed joy.

In public use, things are not much better with the noun "glory." Like any stock phrase, "the power and the glory" does not say much to the ordinary person on the street. And the expression "all the glory" means whatever it needs to mean. The term has taken on an ironic, sometimes almost obscene connotation. Glory has thus been lost to us twice, this second time verbally.

Among the reasons for this loss, beyond normal linguistic degeneration, we should probably reckon in historical circumstances. In the sixteenth century, for example, Luther rejected the *theologia gloriae* for a *theologia crucis*. Nevertheless, whatever the cause of the word's loss of meaning, the result is the same; it is in serious need of revitalization. It has lost its luminosity. Can we restore it?

A good way is to do so is to begin modestly, starting from the realities of the material world. Paul does not hesitate to use concrete images when speaking of our coming resurrection:

"There are both heavenly bodies and earthly bodies, but the glory *(doxa)* of the heavenly is one thing, and that of the earthly is another. There is one glory of the sun, and another glory of the moon, and another glory of the stars; indeed, star differs from star in glory. So it is with the resurrection of the dead. What is sown is perishable, what is raised is imperishable. It is sown in dishonor, it is raised in glory"—*en doxē,* as it reads in Greek (1 Cor 15:40–43).

Following the apostle's lead, we too can proceed from realities we are well acquainted with—perhaps, say, from fascinating meteorological phenomena. It can happen in cloudy weather, for instance, that the sun may suddenly appear from between two thick rain clouds. We see its rays spreading out from it as spokes from the hub of a wheel. Awkwardly perhaps, but in a way that stimulates the imagination, Christian artists have often used gilt wood to represent this phenomenon above an altar, intending to suggest God's brilliant majesty. In the terminology of art history, a work like this is called a *gloire.*

Thanks to such associations with light, we can begin to form an appreciation for what Paul means by the word *doxa,* and thereby begin to restore its former luster. But Paul himself did not coin the word; he inherited it from his Jewish forefathers. Thus, it will be wise review the various Old Testament texts he cites or alludes to in this connection.

GLORY IN THE OLD TESTAMENT

Occasionally in the Old Testament we hear of something that could be called an aesthetic experience. Christ put us on the right track the day he spoke of the lilies of the field. They neither work nor spin, he said. But "even Solomon in all his glory *[doxa]* was not clothed like one of these" (Matt 6:28–29). King Solomon's glory is associated here with majesty and beauty. God's own majesty and beauty are praised in a number of cosmic psalms, among others in Psalm 104, which begins as follows: "Bless the LORD, O my soul. O LORD my God, you are very great. You are clothed with honor and majesty, wrapped in light as with a garment" (Ps 104:1–2).

Sometimes a ravishingly aesthetic experience of a natural phenomenon is mingled with a sprinkling of fear. We see this in Psalm 29, whose author trembles in the face of a thunderstorm. He is so overwhelmed by its fury that he identifies it metaphorically with the voice of God: "The voice of the LORD is powerful; the voice of the LORD is full of majesty. The voice of the LORD breaks the cedars; . . . and in his temple all say, 'Glory!'" (Ps 29:4–5, 9). This frightening phenomenon confronting the poet is comparable to the one the Israelites encountered at the foot of Sinai. "On the morning of the third day there was thunder and lightning, as well as a thick cloud on the mountain, and a blast of a trumpet so loud that all the people who were in the camp trembled" (Exod 19:16). "When all the people witnessed the thunder and lightning, the sound of the trumpet, and the mountain smoking, they were afraid and trembled and stood at a distance, and said to Moses, 'You speak to us, and we will listen; but do not let God speak to us, or we will die'" (Exod 20:18–19). Here again, thunder is interpreted as the voice of God.

Again in Exodus, we see Moses climbing up the mountain by himself to confer with God, and we hear that God "used to speak to Moses face-to-face, as one speaks to a friend" (Exod 33:11). This image, of course, is not meant to be taken literally; rather it is a poetic expression of the strange familiarity between God and Moses. But this familiar intercourse was not one without risk. One day, at the top of this imposing mass of rock, Moses made bold to ask God for the thing that stood highest on his wish-list: "Show me your glory, I pray" (Exod 33:18). The Lord answered him mercifully: You do not know what you are saying! If I grant your request, you are a dead man! And in the words of the Bible:

> "I will make all my goodness pass before you, . . . [but] you cannot see my face; for no one shall see me and live." And the LORD continued, "See, there is a place by me where you shall stand on the rock; and while my glory passes by I will put you in a cleft of the rock, and I will cover you with my hand until I have passed by; then I will take away my hand, and you shall see my back; but my face shall not be seen." (Exod 33:19–23)

The glory of the Lord, then, while fascinating with regard to "majesty," is at the same time gravely dangerous. It is both something to delight in and something to tremble at, truly a *mysterium tremendum et fascinosum.* This ambivalent effect is the subject of several texts, among them those in which one prophet or another relates the circumstances of his call.

Especially rich in this connection is Ezekiel's account, a text of profound literary dignity. What the prophet witnesses, beside the River Chebar, is so overwhelming that language is rendered nearly useless to him for describing it. Ezekiel is so smitten by the peculiar things he sees that he is reduced to using multiple approximations, qualifications, and reservations:

> As I looked, a stormy wind came out of the north: a great cloud with brightness around it and fire flashing forth continually, and in the middle of the fire, something like gleaming amber. In the middle of it was something like four living creatures. . . . each of them had four wings.
>
> In the middle of the living creatures there was something that looked like burning coals of fire, like torches moving to and fro among the living creatures; . . . Over the heads of the living creatures there was something like a dome, shining like crystal, spread out above their heads.

When they moved, I heard the sound of their wings like the sound of mighty waters, like the thunder of the Almighty, a sound of tumult like the sound of an army . . .

And above the dome over their heads there was something like a throne, in appearance like sapphire; and seated above the likeness of a throne was something that seemed like a human form. Upward from what appeared like the loins I saw something like gleaming amber, something that looked like fire enclosed all around; and downward from what looked like the loins I saw something that looked like fire, and there was a splendor all around. Like the bow in a cloud on a rainy day, such was the appearance of the splendor all around. This was the appearance of the likeness of the glory of the LORD. When I saw it, I fell on my face. (Ezek 1:4–6, 13, 22, 24, 26–28)

Through repeated use of phrases such as "something like," "something that looked like," "in appearance like," "something that seemed like," the prophet indicates both the similarity and the dissimilarity between the heavenly world and the earthly one he has experienced. By both bringing them together and keeping them distinct, he tries to make language exceed itself, for the simple reason that the realities he is attempting to describe exceed themselves as well. They are what they are, but not only what they are. Or perhaps better said: they are what they are to the eminent degree; they exceed every conceivable counterpart in our experience. The final impression is one of a massive superiority that leads Ezekiel the seer to throw himself facedown in the dust.

Every time a chosen person comes into close contact with the Lord, that person is caught up in both rapture and panic. Trembling, he falls to the ground, like Ezekiel, or hides his face with his mantle, like Elijah in the cave (1 Kgs 19:13). At the very least he cries out, "Woe is me! I am lost!" as Isaiah does after seeing the Lord seated on a throne, high and lofty, and hearing the seraphs calling to one another, "The whole earth is full of his glory!" (Isa 6:1–5). The Greek word *doxa,* as well as its Hebrew equivalent *kabod,* is thus heavily loaded. It is a word deserving to be written in fire.

The glory of God, manifested in shocking natural phenomena and in strange visions, also manifests itself in historical events, sometimes called "the Lord's great works" or his "mighty deeds." Foremost among them, and most vivid in the collective memory of the Hebrew people, was their liberation from Egypt, narrated in the Book of Exodus. The author depicts the Lord a promising, "I will gain glory for myself over Pharaoh and all his army" (Exod 14:4). Then, after passing through the Red Sea, Moses and the children of Israel sing a lengthy song of victory, which runs, in part, as follows: "Your right hand, O LORD, glorious in power—your right hand, O LORD, shattered the enemy. In the greatness of your majesty you overthrew your adversaries" (15:6–7).

The word "glory," referring to God's enormous strength, his powerful majesty, and his breathtaking radiance, is truly a key word in the Old Testament. Well acquainted with these texts was the man who represented himself as "circumcised on the eighth day, a member of the people of Israel, of the tribe of Benjamin, a Hebrew born of Hebrews" (Phil 3:5). What special meaning did he place in this traditional concept of glory?

THE GLORY OF THE FATHER

This Hebrew, this Israelite and descendant of Abraham (2 Cor 11:22), this man who was first called Saul, received from Gamaliel a fundamental education in the hereditary Jewish law (Acts 22:3). Later he boasted that he had lived in accordance with Judaism's strictest sect (26:5). If we read his letters carefully, we can see that he actually was faithful to the traditional teachings. For him, too, glory was a characteristic belonging to God alone.

As early as 1 Thessalonians, he speaks of the God who calls believers into "his" glory (1 Thess 2:12). In 2 Corinthians, he speaks of "the glory of God" (2 Cor 4:6). Similarly in Romans: what sinful humanity has exchanged for idols, as we hear in the beginning of the letter, is nothing less than "the glory of the immortal God" (Rom 1:23). A little further on we read that owing to this failure of trust, the human race has lost precisely this "glory of God" (3:23). But when we have been brought again through faith into fellowship with him, we nourish the hope of sharing in this "glory of God" (5:2). And then both the first major section of Romans and the epistle as a whole are rounded off with a doxology in the words, "to him be the glory forever, amen" (11:36 and 16:27).

Sometimes the matter is made more precise, in a direction deviating somewhat from Judaism. We hear of "the Father's glory." According to Luke's report of the first Christian Pentecost, Jews and proselytes both adopted Old Testament formulas to speak of "God's deeds of power" (Acts 2:11). But the foremost of these deeds, in their eyes no less than in Paul's, was that Christ had been raised from the dead "by the glory of the Father," as it is expressed in Romans 6:4. In other words, Christ was raised through a brilliant manifestation of God's power. This is echoed by Paul's close disciple, who prays that "the Father of glory" (Eph 1:17) will enlighten the eyes of his readers' heart, so that they can see "what is the immeasurable greatness of his power for [them, the same great power that God worked] in Christ when he raised him from the dead and seated him at his right hand in the heavenly places" (vv. 19–20). A bit further on he offers another prayer to God, asking this time that "according to the riches of his glory, he may grant that [they] may be strengthened in [their] inner being with power" (3:16). In the Pauline corpus, then, glory is an attribute of the Father. But does this mean that no one else shares in it? What about the Son?

THE GLORY OF CHRIST

In his first letter to Corinth, Paul claims, with rhetorical exaggeration, that he has determined to know nothing other than Christ crucified (1 Cor 2:2)—in other words, nothing else than Christ disgraced. Yet only a few verses later, in the same pericope about God's mysterious wisdom, he presents Christ as not only disgraced, but exalted as well: "None of the rulers of this age understood this; for if they had, they would not have crucified the Lord of glory" (v. 8). "Lord of glory": two heavily weighted words that in the Old Testament sometimes refer to Yahweh.

Here in 1 Corinthians Paul does not take the matter any further. But he does indeed do so in his second letter to Corinth (2 Cor 3:7–4:6). There, among other things, he writes, "And even if our gospel is veiled, it is veiled to those who are perishing. In their case the god of this world [the devil] has blinded the minds of the unbelievers, to keep them from seeing the light of the gospel of the glory of Christ, who is the image of God. For we do not proclaim ourselves; we proclaim Jesus Christ as Lord and ourselves as your slaves for Jesus' sake. For it is the God who said, 'Let light shine out of darkness,' who has shone in our hearts to give the light of the knowledge of the glory of God in the face of Jesus Christ" (2 Cor 4:3–6). It is clear from the parallelism between "the gospel of the glory of Christ" and "the knowledge of the glory of God" that they have something in common with each other. Precisely because of his final revelation, the Risen One is presented as an image and a reflection of God's own glory. He is the perfect icon of the Father.

This "icon" has drawn the attention of several biblical writers. It is as if they can not get enough of him: "he is the image of the invisible God" (Col 1:15); he "is the reflection of God's glory and the exact imprint of God's very being" (Heb 1:3). As long as we wander upon the face of the earth, there can be no loftier object for our contemplation.

OUR OWN GLORY

We have just seen, in 1 Cor 2:2–8, how Paul contrasts the death of Christ with Christ's exaltation through being raised from the dead. A similar contrast appears in Romans, but this time it applies to us: "if children, then heirs, heirs of God and joint heirs with Christ—if, in fact, we suffer with him so that we may also [later] be glorified with him" (Rom 8:17). Clearly this coming reality is very often associated with Christ. Thus in Philippians we read, "But our citizenship is in heaven, and it is from there that we are expecting a Savior, the Lord Jesus Christ. He will transform the body of our humiliation that it may be conformed to the body of his glory, by the power that also enables him to make all things subject to himself" (Phil 3:20–21).

That is how Philippians puts it. But nowhere in the Pauline corpus are Christ and the hope of glory so intimately associated as they are in the letter to the Colossians. There we read of what is "laid up for [the readers] in heaven" (Col 1:5). These readers are then urged to give "thanks to the Father, who has enabled [them] to share in the inheritance of the saints in the light" (v. 12). And further on, speaking of the revealed mystery, the author tells his audience that "God chose to make known how great among the Gentiles are the riches of the glory of this mystery, which is Christ in you, the hope of glory"

(v. 27). It is this very hope that looms in the background later
on in the letter: "When Christ who is your life is revealed, then
you also will be revealed with him in glory" (Col 3:4).

The apostle's intimate circle, then, was convinced that we
shall one day be glorified. But are we actually glorified already?
There are at least two texts that throw light on this question,
and both belong among the key passages on the subject: 2 Corinthians 3:7–4:6 and Romans 8:17–30.

In the first of these texts, Paul reminds his readers that
Moses was compelled to cover his face with a veil "to keep the
people of Israel from gazing at the end of the [reflection of di-
vine] glory that was being set aside" (2 Cor 3:13). He then
claims that a veil still hangs over the faces of later Israelites
(vv. 14–15)—metaphorically speaking—while the veil cover-
ing the faces of Christians is taken away once they turn in faith
to Christ (v. 16). Paul summarizes in verse 18: "And all of us,
with unveiled faces, seeing [present tense] the glory of the Lord
as though reflected in a mirror, are being transformed [present
tense again] into the same image from one degree of glory to
another." In this way, Paul describes a process that is taking
place now, here on earth.

The second text, which makes it clear that this process has
already begun, runs as follows: "We know that all things work
together for good for those who love God, who are called according to his purpose. For those whom he foreknew he also
predestined to be conformed to the image of his Son, in order
that he might be the firstborn within a large family. . . . [And
them] he also glorified" (Rom 8:28–30). The unexpected past
tense—an aorist in fact—is confusing. Still, it must surely
imply that we are dealing here with something that has already

been achieved, at least in part. But what can Paul have meant by being "conformed to the image of his Son"?

"... TO BE CONFORMED TO THE IMAGE OF HIS SON"

To describe our relationship to God we often use such moral categories as sin and forgiveness, enmity and reconciliation, and so forth. Paul does this, too, sometimes. Yet more often than we realize, he also uses other categories: visual and even aesthetic categories. One feature of his writings, all too seldom observed, is their frequent use of such words as light, appearance, reflection, radiance, image, copy, likeness, face, change, metamorphosis, and the like. These words are related to one another in that they all can connote something beautiful and noble, something positive. But what do they actually have to do with each other? Of course, we can bring them together, experimentally or playfully, even ironically, as when we say that someone beholds her face in a mirror and sees, at best, something beautiful. This works in a secular context, of course. But what sort of semantic connection exists among these words in Paul's mind?

Clearly the most frequent of them are "image" and "copy," as for example in regard to humanity's fall and rehabilitation. When the apostle says that the sinful race has "fall[en] short of the glory of God" (Rom 3:23), we may reasonably understand him to mean that previously the race possessed that glory. Probably behind this text is the story in Genesis, according to which the original humans were created "in the image of God" (Gen 1:27), created "according to [God's] likeness" (v. 26). Humanity's purpose was thus to reflect in their own faces the face of God himself.

But we know how things turned out. Human beings, individually and collectively, "knew God, [but] did not honor him as God" (Rom 1:21). "They exchanged the glory of the immortal God for images resembling a mortal human being or birds or four-footed animals or reptiles" (v. 23; here Paul links up with Old Testament writers who ridicule cults and images of false gods). Or, summing up all that he has said so far: "They exchanged the truth about God for a lie and worshiped and served the creature rather than the Creator, who is blessed forever! Amen" (v. 25).

But we cannot disfigure the image of God without consequences. Through the discrepancy between what we know and what we do, we disfigure ourselves at the same time. Thanks to a kind of spiritual schizophrenia, a person's very face ceases to be recognizable. Through being inconsistent people have become distorted from what they were intended to be. Paul insists, "They became futile in their thinking, and their senseless minds were darkened. Claiming to be wise, they became fools" (vv. 21–22). They had been intended to reflect God's flawless beauty, but as a result of their internal rift, the mirror shattered. The loss of integrity entailed that God could no longer recognize his own features in this person, in what from time to time Paul calls "the old nature." All that was left for God to do was to start from the ground up and bring forth a new humanity made in "the image of its creator" (Col 3:9–10), or as Ephesians puts it, "created according to the likeness of God" (Eph 4:23–24). Is this re-creation carried out directly, or is it done through an intermediary image or model instead?

Of course there was at least one person who truly was an "image of God," namely Christ (2 Cor 4:4). He is thus the only one who can function as the prototype for the new humanity, the "firstborn within a large family" (Rom 8:29b). God's work of re-creation consists then in conforming human beings "to the image of his Son" (v. 29a). It is not easy to translate the adjective Paul uses here: *symmorphous*. It begins with the prefix *sym-*, which we render with such English morphemes as *co-*, *con-*, or *like-*, all of which refer to a kind of symbiosis. We might translate *symmorphous* with the phrase "similarly formed," which indicates a transformation leading to a completely obvious family relationship.

God's dearest wish is that we, his adopted children, might come to resemble the one who is the Son par excellence. Put another way, God's ultimate plan can be described as aiming to restore humanity, just as an art expert slowly and carefully restores a damaged portrait, or as a plastic surgeon returns to a disfigured face its former beauty. And the model the divine surgeon follows in bringing about this transformation is Christ, his very own image.

Of course, fully manifested likeness with him is still a dream of the future, though something we are nonetheless destined for. Speaking of our coming resurrection, Paul assures his readers that we will "bear the image of the man of heaven," that is, of the new Adam, the risen Christ (1 Cor 15:49). Meanwhile that likeness can be gradually realized here on earth. The apostle has given equally firm assurances that by regarding the glory of God reflected in the face of Christ, we are already being changed into his image (2 Cor 3:18).

Truly *doxa* is the ultimate word for what Paul means when he speaks of God and of our participation in the divine. In order to make this word shine even more clearly in our eyes and to make the reality it refers to even more attractive, we can conclude our exercise in looking forward by observing how the apostle characterizes that reality.

THE PECULIAR NATURE OF DIVINE GLORY

When Paul writes about divine wisdom, he uses only negatives. Sometimes he praises God because God alone is wise, literally incomparable. Other times he is carried away by the thought that God's wisdom is deep, unsearchable, unfathomable, even to the point of boldly depicting it as an un-wisdom, as foolishness. Whenever he deals with this divine attribute, all he can do is to deny, and deny, and deny again. Though he does so through various literary means, he always does it with the same radical force. But how does he handle a different divine attribute, the attribute of glory? Some texts are so rich that we willingly return to them, fully assured that they still have more to offer us. One such text is the following, addressed to the Corinthians:

> [God] has made us competent to be ministers of a new covenant, not of letter but of spirit; . . . Now if the ministry of death, chiseled in letters on stone tablets, came in glory so that the people of Israel could not gaze at Moses' face because of the glory of his face, a glory now set aside, how much more will the ministry of the Spirit come in glory? For if there was glory in the ministry of condemnation, much more does the ministry of justification abound in glory! Indeed, what once had glory has lost its glory because of the greater glory; for if what was set aside came through glory, much more has the permanent come in glory! (2 Cor 3:6–11)

It is striking here how frequently Paul compares corresponding realities: two kinds of service, two covenants, two successive manifestations of glory. Comparisons, of course, can go in two directions: they can either bring things together as in some sense equal to one another, or they can show how they differ. In the one case we focus on the similarities, and in the other on the dissimilarities. In this text Paul does both. All

three times he draws a parallel between two things while simultaneously contrasting them; all three times he expresses his
preference for the second, later thing, as somehow better than
the first.

In other words, Paul argues from the small to the great:
"how much more . . . much more does . . . much more has . . ."
The tone is positive, testifying to Paul's mounting admiration.
He moves from affirmation to affirmation, even perhaps to
"super-affirmation." For as a matter of fact he does not actually
argue from the small to the great, but from the smaller to the
greater.

That is, as his point of comparison, he proceeds not from
something insignificant, mediocre, or easily outdone, but from
one of the most highly revered features of Jewish devotional
tradition: the divine radiance reflected in the face of Moses.
There at Sinai we witness perhaps the most remarkably elevating experience in human history. Yet Paul now insists that this
extraordinarily exalted event is in fact as good as nothing in
comparison to "the glory of God in the face of Jesus Christ,"
as he is soon to phrase it (2 Cor 4:6). This new manifestation
of God's outpoured radiance exceeds the former one in two
respects: in part, it is simply more intense (3:7–8); in part, it
is permanent—it endures, contrary to the earlier manifestation that soon faded (v. 11). Thus he summarizes, "Indeed,
what once had glory has lost its glory because of the greater
glory" (v. 10).

This "greater glory" deserves a moment's further reflection. We do not always choose our every word when we speak;
sometimes we use fixed formulations, even if they do not exactly reflect our intended meaning. It can even happen that we

let the tongue run free, so to speak, without our cooperation, and let it utter innocent but meaningless exaggerations, such as "I am completely exhausted" or "I am unendingly grateful," and so on. These little linguistic indulgences are treacherous. They leave us jaded, making it hard for us to take seriously authors who really mean what they do say.

Paul truly means what he says in this text about the overwhelming superiority of the divine glory in the face of Christ; his words here do not just slide mechanically off his lips. This is obvious from the fact that he very soon uses the same exaggerated tone in a new comparison. This time he speaks of the present and the future: "For this slight momentary affliction is preparing us for an eternal weight of glory beyond all measure" (4:17). Thus, in his mind there is no attributive strong enough to evoke the richness of the glory that lies far beyond all our meager experiences of abundance.

He speaks of richness, and of weight. The text we just now cited reads like this in the King James Version: "For our light affliction, which is but for a moment, worketh for us a far more exceeding and eternal weight of glory" (2 Cor 4:17). Paul is so overwhelmed, so overpowered by this disproportion in glory that he returns to it in Romans: "I consider that the sufferings of this present time are not worth comparing with the glory about to be revealed to us" (Rom 8:18).

The Greek phrase translated here as "worth comparing" originally connoted weightlessness. It thus corresponds to the word "slight" (or the King James Version's "light") in the Corinthian text. In both Romans and 2 Corinthians, Paul experiences glory as an inconceivably great weight. In this he actually follows in the footsteps of his fathers. In the Old Testament the

Hebrew term *kabod* pointed to precisely this thought of weight, mass. It was first applied to the importance of a wealthy, powerful man, to his weighty authority, before it came to be used of God himself and his own majesty.

"DEEP CALLS TO DEEP . . ."

We may now review the entire field and see how Paul carries out the practice of looking backward and forward, respectively. For him it is the difference between looking to the origin of things and to their goal. When he goes historically upstream, toward God's wisdom, toward the source of God's redeeming act, motivated as it was by his undeserved mercy, Paul claims to stand in the presence of an unfathomable mystery. When he turns downstream, toward the fulfillment of God's plan of salvation, he stands again before a similarly deep mystery. In the wake of grateful memories of what God has done in the past comes an eager, curious anticipation of what God will do in the future. Paul rejoices in advance over the promised vision of God's beauty. But looking backward or forward, he finds himself confronted by something defying our ability to understand. Deep calls to deep.

Meanwhile, he employs two types of literary moves. In the one case he eliminates every conceivable comparison. In the other, he compares with decisive intent. He moves from the lesser to the greater. He draws parallels between two things, but always with a preference for the later one; his orientation is always toward the future. He goes from affirmation to affirmation, even to superaffirmation. That is, he multiplies superlative adjectives: "overwhelming," "beyond knowledge." He uses comparative formulations: "how much greater . . . ," "how much richer . . . ," and he avails himself of hyperbolic phrases that exceed the limits of normal linguistic usage: "an eternal weight of glory beyond all measure . . ." or "not worthy to be compared with . . ." In this way he preserves the exalted mysteriousness of God, while at the same time being bold enough to say something about it.

Thus he is unceasingly working himself up to a climax. This very upward mounting scale is what Thomas Aquinas meant by the *via eminentiae*. God truly does possess glory, and he does so to an eminent degree.